A Voice Reborn

Kyra Vayne

'Truly beautiful ... all the qualities you want of a grand operatic voice [with] a remarkable technique'
– Norman Lebrect, *Niteline*, ABC News

'It was a big enough thrill discovering your wonderful CD, and sharing that with my listeners. I have been very excited by the "rediscovery". And I know that such excitement is shared by many others. I do hope that this burst of long overdue fondness for your glorious voice makes you happy! It is certainly having that effect on a lot of other people' – Brian Kay

'A remarkable testiment of a singing technique'
– BBC *Today Programme*

'One of the finest singers this century ... CDs of Kyra Vayne's historic performances, auditions and broadcasts have been released to tumultuous response' – *The Lady*

'Not to be missed! Undoubtedly the equal of many of the greatest singers from the "Golden Era" [with] a truly luscious timbre'
– *Record Collector*

'The perfect voice of its generation. I was struck by the virtuosity of this singer who really could do anything she liked with the aria. There are no two ways about it: here was a phenomenon – the voice had a life of its own' – *The Singer*

'Impassioned, full-voiced ... with plenty of dramatic fire' – *Opera*

'She took the theatre by storm. Her voice stamps her as our newest prima donna' – *News of the World*

'A dramatic soprano with a beautifully rounded powerful voice ... her notes float out on velvet' – *Yorkshire Post*

'A voice like shot silk, with sheen and depth and unsuspected colours' – *Globe and Mail*

'A jolly good singer ... absolutely perfect' – Vilem Tauski

A Voice Reborn

KYRA VAYNE

WITH ANDREW PALMER

Foreword by Sue Lawley

ARCADIA BOOKS
LONDON

Arcadia Books Ltd
15–16 Nassau Street
London WIN 7RE

First published in Great Britain 1999
© Kyra Vayne 1999

A catalogue record for this book is available
from the British Library.

ISBN 1–900850–27–3

Typeset in Scala and Scala Sans by Discript, London WC2N 4BL
Printed in Finland by WSOY

Arcadia Books distributors are as follows:
in the UK and elsewhere in Europe:
Turnaround Publishers Services
Unit 3, Olympia Trading Estate
Coburg Road
London N22 6TZ

in the USA and Canada:
Consortium Book Sales and Distribution, Inc.
1045 Westgate Drive
St Paul, MN 55114–1065

in Australia:
Tower Books
PO Box 213
Brookvale, NSW 2100

in New Zealand:
Addenda
Box 78224
Grey Lynn
Auckland

in South Africa:
Peter Hyde Associates (Pty) Ltd
PO Box 2856
Cape Town 8000

Contents

Acknowledgements

I would like to offer my warmest thanks to the many friends who have given me continuing support and encouragement during the last few years. I am particularly grateful to Patrick Bade, Peter and Anne Chappell, Richard Copeman, Colin Dean, Cynthia Edwards, Rita Grudzien, Peter Hillier, Gina Jannis, Mark Jones, Peter Jukes, Griselda La Roche, Helma Okin and her son Earl, Alberto Portugeis, Jo and Kathy Robinson, Richard Samuel, Tsivi Sharret, Hilary Stafford-Clarke, Colin Tilney, Christopher Walker and Philip Woods. Each of them knows the ways in which he or she has helped me, and in each case it has meant a great deal to me.

Most of all, however, I give my retrospective thanks to the late Boris Nadan. It was he, with such good intentions, who motivated my 'rebirth'. Without him this book could not have been written.

Foreword

I met Kyra Vayne when she came to tell me about her life on Radio Four's *Desert Island Discs*. Now in her eighties, the woman who's been called 'opera's forgotten voice' is still as compelling as she must have been in her heyday – and probably just as mischievous.

Born in Russia before the Revolution, she knew poverty and hardship, but the gift of a beautiful voice brought her fame and success. At the height of her career she sang with Gigli, Gobbi, and Bergonzi, but then disaster struck. Forced to abandon her life as an opera diva, she spent her middle years working anonymously as a secretary. Her glamorous past was never mentioned – except that a clairvoyant told her that her voice would one day be 'reborn'.

'The voice', as Kyra calls it, stayed with her – if only in the form of ancient tape recordings which she kept under a bed in her West London flat. When they were finally unearthed and published in the 1990s, the forecast came true – the musical world once again took notice of Kyra Vayne. And quite right too. Hers is a glorious voice which glides effortlessly through the most demanding arias.

I often play her 'Letter Scene' from Tchaikovsky's *Eugene Onegin* in which, as Tatyana, she captures the desperation of first love. As she told me, 'Tatyana is the embodiment of the Russian girl – the pure soul of Russia.' Reading the story of Kyra's life, and hearing her sing, make one think that this must be as true of the singer as it is of the character she so loved to play.

I'm delighted that *Desert Island Discs* has helped to bring the name of Kyra Vayne back to public attention, and I'm sure that many people will be fascinated to read this, the story of her extraordinary life.

Sue Lawley
September 1999

The Prophecy

I N 1963, six years after being forced to give up my singing career, I was involved in a futureless and rather depressing relationship with a Russian engineer who had had a very serious operation just before we met. My feelings towards him were of great affection, coupled with an enormous desire to see him cleared of the cancer from which he had nearly died. But although he professed the most ardent love for me, he seemed incapable of relating to me, and all my feelings were being slowly stifled by his continuing annihilation of me as a person.

A friend suggested that I consult a spiritualist who had apparently been a great help to many people. She duly came to see me and, although knowing nothing about me, gave an excellent reading of my past and of the current situation and its imminent development – which, I was told, would at last leave me free. Then, as she was about to leave, she stopped in her tracks for a moment and seemed to go into a slight trance. Her glance went past me into the distance, and she said in a flat voice, 'When you are at the end of your life and your voice is but a memory, and your career is forgotten, your voice will be reborn.' Then she left.

The unexpectedness and incongruity of what she said imprinted itself on my mind forever. Naturally, I did not for one moment take her message literally, and whenever the memory of her words came out of my brain-box for a dusting, I became more convinced of their mystical connotation which, perhaps at my death, I would understand but which, at present, eluded me.

More than thirty years later her prophecy became a reality. It *did* come true, and in a far wider way than anyone could ever have imagined.

The Beginning

M Y FAMILY'S HISTORY is more complicated than most, and I therefore request the indulgence of readers while I explain how I came into the world. And explain it I must, for it was to have a very important bearing on the rest of my life.

My maternal grandfather was Edmund Von Der Beek, one of many Baltic barons. His wife, my grandmother, was an American whom he wooed on his three trips to the United States – and eventually won. Edmund's sister Elizabeth married Max Knopmuss, who was also of Russo-Germanic stock, and they lived in a very beautiful flat in St Petersburg's Nevsky Prospect. Their son, born in 1876 and also called Max, was my father, and therefore my parents were first cousins.

My mother, Maria, was born in 1874 and first met Father when he visited her family in Moscow. They were both in their teens and fell in love at first sight, much to the horror of both families. Father was immediately sent home in disgrace, and after finishing his education and serving his apprenticeship at Brandt's, an international private bank, he was despatched to its London branch as soon as possible in order to save the family further embarrassment. Mother stayed behind in Moscow and remained unmarried for many years.

When she was twenty-five – at that time virtually 'on the shelf' – she married a charismatic and attractive Frenchman, Kurt Eberlein. He was apparently a professional gambler to whom nothing seemed to matter except winning – something he never did. They had two children: Alice, born in 1900, and Vera, born two years later. The marriage was a disaster, and after ten years it ended abruptly when the bailiffs cleared their home of all the furniture. In disgrace, Mother was forced to return to her parents.

At about this time Max Knopmuss, my paternal grandfather, lost his shirt on the stock exchange, and very soon afterwards he died of a heart attack. He left behind a widow, three unmarried daughters and two sons; and Father, the elder son by eleven years, had no choice but to return to Russia from London to take on the responsibility of looking after the family. Learning of Mother's sad plight in Moscow, he took on an even greater weight by writing to her and advising that she obtain a divorce and marry him as soon as possible. Mother had no better options, and in any case still loved him, so she did as he suggested.

Soon after her divorce from Kurt Eberlein she arrived in St Petersburg, with her two children, to marry Father. They all moved into my grandmother's flat and, not surprisingly, there was enormous enmity from the ranks of the Knopmuss relatives towards Mother. This marriage, too, was not exactly made in heaven; and inevitably, I suppose, it foundered badly from the start. Alice loathed Father from the word go, resenting him and unfairly blaming him for the loss of her own father. Sadly, her sister Vera died of leukaemia in 1910 at the age of eight. Two years later my sister Maya came into the world, and I, Kyra Knopmuss, was born on 29 January 1916. Within eighteen months all hell was let loose, and life in Russia changed forever – the Revolution saw to that.

*

My family had a small dacha in **Teriokki**, a summer getaway and winter ski resort on the border of Russia and Finland, within easy reach of St Petersburg. In the short period between my birth and the start of the Revolution we spent a summer there. Our neighbour was none other than Trotsky, and I was told that he carried me very affably in his arms, making all the right noises; but he is *not* someone who I personally would choose to be cooed over by.

*

At the beginning of the Revolution, Father was the director of an important horseshoe factory, and he therefore became an immediate target. When rumours of an 'inspection' by the Bolsheviks became an imminent reality, the factory's employees, with whom Father was very popular, came up with a danger-proof escape plan for him. He and his chauffeur would exchange clothes, and while Father left the building by the back entrance the chauffeur would make his exit from the front. It was assumed that the chauffeur would be arrested, after which his identity would be discovered and he would be released immediately. Instead, the Bolsheviks stormed the building and shot at point-blank range the man whom they took to be my father. One can only imagine what this appalling incident did to Father, who was anything but a coward.

By now the passion of my parents' teenage romance had long since faded, for Father's offer to marry Mother had been an act of great gallantry and he had not realized what living together would entail. In fact they divorced three times, for during and immediately after the Revolution, this could be done simply by signing a

4

piece of paper. Although they always returned to each other, Father was never able to rid himself of the frustration that the marriage caused him, and he remained at heart the confirmed bachelor he had been before 'tying the knot'.

Unlike many White Russians who fled immediately to Western Europe, Father was convinced that the Revolution would last for only about six months. So, after depositing in the bank what valuables we had, he decided to take our family south towards the Black Sea. Some time later the banks issued warnings to all customers that if their possessions were not collected by a certain date, everything would be confiscated by the government. By then, however, the mail service had ceased to exist, and so we never received the notification. Even if we had, there would have been no way of rescuing our valuables.

The confusion of the civil war soon became indescribable, and we were continuously caught between the Whites retreating and the Reds attacking, with the partisans (or Greens) bringing up the rear. As the occupants of nearby towns and villages fled, we and many other Whites escaping from St Petersburg (now known as Petrograd) took over as squatters until the next wave of enemy and civilians flushed us out and moved us on.

We squatted in many strange places, and in extraordinary conditions: a butcher's shop, its walls sodden with the blood of long-departed carcasses, where Mother laid me to sleep on a wooden trunk with a curved lid; a villa whose gardens were still immaculate and contained pergolas heavy-laden with vines of 'ladies finger' grapes; and a small farm with abandoned cattle still grazing in the fields. In the farmhouse we discovered cupboards full of grain left by the owners as they fled; and we were left open-mouthed when a pig, revelling in its new-found freedom, suddenly smashed through the glass door of one of the cupboards in search of a feast.

The further we travelled, the more tattered our clothes became. The one luxury that my mother had grabbed when leaving Petrograd was a full-length Persian lamb coat, and in the end this had to be bartered for a single reel of white cotton – a priceless commodity at that time. All these impressions must have influenced my outlook and character, however early they impacted upon my life. But it is hard for me to say how much I actually remember from my early childhood, because so much may be hearsay absorbed into my memory. Things recounted took on a life of their own that nothing would ever obliterate, even though they belong to another, distant life.

Two particular incidents that were told to me became etched on my memory forever. I heard about a diver who was sent to search for something in the River Neva; he went down a young man and came up aged and completely changed. He had been confronted by a forest of corpses apparently standing on the river bed, weighed down with rocks and lashed by the feet to row upon row of tram-lines. I also remember hearing that if two or three people stood together in the street and chatted innocently, the militia would appear from nowhere, sharply pull them apart, and question them closely as to what their conversation had been about. If the separate accounts did not tally exactly – as they were almost certainly bound not to – the 'offenders' would all be sent straight to Siberia, with no second chance of proving their innocence.

We eventually reached Anapa in the Crimea, but by this time I was gravely ill with dysentery – the price of semi-starvation – and was not expected to live. I can remember reaching the outskirts of the town and having my 'last' photo taken while holding a rusk – the only available food that I could digest. A doctor told Father that the only thing that could save me was a boiling hot mustard bath. This was a traditional Russian remedy for cholera and other ende-mic diseases rife during that period; it stimulated the circulation and thus raised the temperature of the body. When Father asked where he could obtain mustard he was told, 'That's *your* problem.' Notwithstanding empty shops and a strict curfew, he somehow succeeded in procuring some, and the hot mustard bath saved my life.

Since the fighting in the civil war had by now died down a little, Father decided to make the journey back to Petrograd as soon as possible. He therefore continued on his way while Mother, Maya and I stayed near Moscow to be near my half-sister, Alice. She was working for the American Red Cross and could, we hoped, be of some help to us, however small. We found some appalling accommodation in Leonosovo, a tiny village outside the city where, after a while, Mother was able to exploit her musical talents by giving piano lessons to the children of once-wealthy families who had evacuated to their country dachas at the out-break of the Revolution and who were living a relatively normal existence.

For us, however, conditions in and around Moscow were horrific, with little food or clothing. I vividly remember Mother setting off on one of her lengthy treks in soggy, snowy, marshy ground in midwinter; her leaking shoes were reinforced with newspaper and tied together with string, and she wore a long multicoloured shawl crocheted together out of odd bits of wool. Maya, although only three and a half years my senior, was already nearly an adult; she had seen and understood so much more of the horrors around us than I, and by the age of eight she had joined the local tribe of delinquents, spending her days on forays of plunder and the survival of the fittest.

I was therefore left alone in the village for days at a time, standing on the spot where I had tearfully kissed Mother goodbye, and waiting for her beloved figure to emerge over the horizon. She would sometimes be paid in kind – usually with a meal of some sort – and if this were the case she would take me with her. But once we had reached our destination I would plant myself by the railings outside the house, and wild horses would not budge me. The reason was simple: I was terrified, beyond all explanation, of strangers. And poor Mother would choke on food when offered it, knowing that nothing would or could force me to join her or swallow whatever little there was to eat.

These experiences of being separated from her so traumatized me that I grew to fear the piano because of what it had stood for, and I never learned to play it. Mother did try to teach me when I was older, but unfortunately she vented all the frustrations caused by her other pupils on *me*, taking a ruler or pencil and slapping my fingers when I made a mistake. Piano lessons soon became a torment for me, and poor Mother never really understood why she could not teach me when she had been successful with so many other children. She eventually admitted defeat and gave up, but it took me years to understand why I had once been so averse to learning music theory.

✳

Not long ago I had the pleasure of meeting a delightful Russian lady from Moscow, and while chatting, I idly asked her if she knew of Leonosovo. To my amazement, she replied that it is no longer a grim little village but an affluent district of the capital. She added, however, that delinquency is still its trademark. Even more recently, and for some extraordinary reason, the act of writing about this part of my childhood suddenly unlocked a memory that now flashes through my mind in hues made all the more vivid by the suffering and grimness of that period. After more than seventy-five years a shaft of light and a flash of colour now pierce the gloom, and I see, amidst ghastly chaos, the wonderful traditions of Russia continuing regardless: the rituals of a village wedding unfold like a

2

Childhood in Petrograd

I F ONLY one could remember one's life consecutively, like a huge tapestry, instead of miscellaneous and sometimes unrelated incidents! Yet whatever one remembers is precious and fragile, and must be treated with care in case it disappears from memory.

After we were reunited with Father in Petrograd, there was an artificial lull in the conflict of the civil war. Very slowly, things started to get back to normal, or as near normal as they could be. We rented a very pleasant flat on one of the islands adjoining the city, and hope seemed to be in the air. My sister Maya went to school and started learning English and German, but unfortunately I was unable to go with her, as schooling did not begin until the age of eight. Life in Petrograd, during those few short years between the old and the new, must have been enormously exciting for a child of my tender age. Strange that, among the chaos that the city must have been in, it had somehow retained an amazing gentility that was ready to come to life as if by the wave of some magic wand.

Is this why, so many years later, I still remember my visits to the celebrated pâtisserie called Lor, in the Nevsky Prospect, which had miraculously survived the Revolution and been restored to its former glory? Its cakes and tarts were legendary, and I used to eat them, clutched in a gloved hand, standing by the shop's counter – this when I was six years old. For a child who had grown up without sugar, which was completely non-existent for several years and which had been replaced by saccharine, this treat was even greater. I obviously had a sweet tooth, and often licked at a bottle of liquid saccharine to satisfy it.

Ice cream was another miracle. The Russian variety was, and still is, beyond compare – cranberry was my favourite flavour. Street vendors would scoop a portion of ice cream onto a paper saucer with a miniature long-handled soup ladle, and I would stand riveted to the spot, determined to have a full scoop by fair means or foul. The great danger was that I might follow, anywhere, any stranger who offered me this delicacy. I sometimes did!

Mother, altruistic as ever, continued to give piano lessons to all and sundry. Her payments were, as always, individual – one particular pupil arrived with something alive and kicking, wrapped in a towel, and presented it to her. It turned out to be an enchanting baby goat, just a few weeks old. Naturally, I was entranced by it, but my joy was short-lived: the animal sucked frenziedly on anything in sight and kicked out with its hind legs in exuberant abandon, smashing everything, targeted or otherwise. So it had to go – where, I never knew.

My father had procured a very individual way of traversing the city in midwinter. I have never seen anything like it since, and I feel that it may have been an exclusive model made to his own design. It was a high chair with armrests, mounted on metal strips of about three yards long, like rails, which glided over ice and snow. I would sit in it while Father put his left foot on the left strip and propelled us with his right. The exhilaration of swishing down the icy road between traffic and pedestrians was enormous for both the privileged passenger and the 'driver'.

Even more exciting was racing across the width of the River Neva, frozen so deeply that the tramlines had been diverted across its surface. The river had thus become a hub of movement and activity. Here and there, a solitary figure could be seen waddling in layers of clothing across the icy surface, sitting on a folding stool, and waiting to plunge a fishing rod into a small hole drilled for the purpose. I remember hearing that fish caught in the river were a great delicacy and were given high-faluting names.

Before the fall of the city, the Royal Arrow Boat Club stood on the banks of the Neva in one of the more salubrious residential areas. At weekends it would be bursting with activity. Many years earlier, my father had been a club member, and when it came back to life in the early 1920s he re-met all his many old sporting cronies there. By this time Maya was a strong swimmer, but I was petrified of water. The Neva had very strong currents, and its many tales of disaster did nothing to take away my fears. To make matters worse, Maya had instilled into me that the sinister-looking black beams that formed breakwaters in the river were actually human souls, transformed as a punishment for their sins. Believe me, she was most convincing when it came to filling me with holy terror.

My father, thwarted by Fate in producing two daughters instead of two sons, was nevertheless determined to make a 'man' of me. And so began the dipping ritual, which I remember to this day with great chagrin. He would hold me by the wrists and dip me into the river, heedless of my panic-stricken screams that soon turned into gurgles of protest, and keep me totally submerged for several seconds. With each dip, I was held underwater for a little longer. This was done in full view of everyone, which for a deeply shy child was sheer hell. The object of the exercise was to teach me to swim, but not surprisingly, the result was exactly the opposite. I do not remember my mother ever being present during those childhood aquatic exercises, and I am sure that she would not have allowed me to be so humiliated.

One of the members of the club was a very colourful character of French extraction, probably in his fifties. He was a fresh air fanatic, and I do not remember him ever being dressed normally – throughout the whole year he wore only a sleeveless vest, shorts, and plimsolls. Even in deepest midwinter, while Father and I were swishing through the town on our lovely chair-sleigh, we would see him jogging along, his whole body a deep purple colour. Not content with this, he had also established the local record for staying underwater and was forever trying to break it.

One day he set out to break his own record once again, my father being one of the observers. He disappeared under the surface of the river for much longer than usual, and Father became agitated, yelling at him to come up. But there was no sign of the record-breaker, and several onlookers dived in after him. After a few minutes they came up with his limp body. He had either been caught in a strong undercurrent that prevented him from surfacing, or had had a heart attack in the water.

This hardly encouraged my interest in swimming, nor did the huge cyclone that I once saw racing towards the banks of the river at great speed. In fact my fear of water has never left me, and to my deep regret, the art of swimming eluded me all my life. Oddly enough, however, I could float. And later in life, as long as there was someone nearby who could help me back onto my feet, I would bob around happily whenever I hit a luxurious *plage* in Europe or elsewhere.

3

Arrival in London

IN 1924 Lenin died, and Stalin took over. Once again, mayhem reigned. An enormous bloodbath was predicted, and Father was warned that he would be on the hit list because, apart from anything else, he had been an officer in the Imperial Army. (Indeed, more than thirty years later army officers were still being assassinated and executed.) We had to leave Russia while we still could – and as discreetly as possible.

Father quickly contacted the London branch of Brandt's where, as a young man, he had been a banker, and was offered a position there. He left first, while Mother and we children stayed behind for a few days to dispose of our possessions. As time was of the essence, she would often beckon to passers-by, invite them into our home, and offer whatever appealed to them since it was of no further use to us.

We were given a permit for only one year, and Father's brother Alec was kept as hostage. When we did not return a year later, he was sent to Siberia. However, he was released after six months due to the fact that he was a highly qualified architect at a time when such a skill was almost non-existent in Russia. A sad postscript to this story is that he, his family, and all our other St Petersburg relatives died an appalling death from starvation during the siege of the city – which was now known as Leningrad. Even the city's cats and dogs were eaten, and in desperation, the last thing my family tried to consume was boiled tree bark.

A couple of weeks after Father's departure for England, we followed by boat. Just before we left, a great friend of the family who was very fond of me presented me with an English ten-shilling note. To me, this was quite magical, even though I had no idea of its value. When our ship stopped at the docks of Kiel Canal and vendors of all sorts came aboard, I went mad and exchanged my precious ten shilling note for a huge box of chocolates, which I ate frenziedly, growling at anyone who came near me. I paid for this indulgence in the obvious way, and it was a very long time before I could look another chocolate in the face!

I vividly remember, on arriving in England, Tower Bridge opening up to allow our ship through into the Port of London – a miraculous sight for a child of eight. The first thing in the city that I can consciously recall seeing was a huge gasometer with *trompe-l'oeil* flames all around it. This filled me with terror. Then I ate my first ever banana and immediately brought it up. We must have been a curious sight: all we had were the clothes we stood up in, and mine were something quite apart – a kind of apron with a far-too-large cardigan enveloping me, and a pair of laced-up, knee-high boots made from sailcloth material, with a tiny heel, of which I was inordinately proud.

We took a large room in St George's Square, Pimlico, where we all lived for a month – in a sort of dream. I was particularly enchanted by the superb private gardens in the square to which local residents gained access by using their own personal keys. Father's salary was forty pounds per month, which was more than adequate to live on comfortably in those days. And yet a different picture emerges when one remembers that things had to be bought in multiples of four, and that many of them wore out at the same time.

Soon after our arrival in London, my half-sister Alice came to visit us. She was married by this time, and although the marriage was not particularly happy and could easily have been disrupted, her continuing resentment and dislike of my father was stronger than our joint pleadings for her to stay in England. After six months she left us, and we went to see her off at the Port of London. It was a bleak and foggy morning, and the sound of the ship's horn hooting its farewell has remained in my memory ever since. For years I kept hearing it, bringing shivers down my back. There was an enormous love between Alice and me, and had she stayed, the pattern of my life would have been completely different. From her I would have received the encouragement that I lacked but so badly needed.

*

Alice had given me several small gifts before she left, including two shillings that had to keep me in 'Dolly Mixture' for twelve days. She also gave me an enchanting miniature tea set, looking like Wedgwood but actually made of papier mâché. It soon became my pride and joy. A couple of days afterwards we were visited by our friends, the Swann family. Dr Swann had been a friend of my father's in St Petersburg, and he and his very beautiful Russo-Persian wife now lived at Elephant and Castle, where he had his surgery. They had a daughter and a son, Donald – yes, he of Flanders and Swann fame. Donald (or Doutik, as he was called) was my junior by about three years, and showed even greater delight in my tiny tea set than I did. In order to express his joy he proceeded to chew every cup and saucer, turning the whole set into a gungy pulp. My parents were too polite to remonstrate, and I was completely stunned by the horror of what was happening. By the time I had gone into action and started to scream, my tea set had dissolved beyond recognition.

Donald had an enchanting lisp and large, innocent, blue eyes made all the larger by his thick spectacle lenses. He was then about five years old, and it was he who accompanied his mother when she sang her gorgeous Russian gypsy songs. He would sit on a piano stool (augmented by three cushions to lift him high enough) and play all those lilting melodies by ear – his talent was quite amazing, and brought him great fame in later years. His career blossomed just at the time that mine crashed, and although I often attended his performances I never went backstage to renew our childhood friendship – I felt such a failure in the light of his enormous success.

When I was about ten years old Mother and I stayed for two weeks in the Swanns' flat in Elephant and Castle, looking after their cat while they were away. A few days after their return, we heard that the cat had fallen off the balcony; and I was totally bewildered when Mrs Swann explained that it had 'committed suicide'. I had always thought that this applied only to humans, and my grief was overwhelming.

✳

Father, always a keen sportsman, took me to watch the 1924 Oxford and Cambridge Boat Race. In those days, the spectators lining the Thames supported their favoured team by buying small celluloid dolls dressed in skirts or tutus of dark blue silk for Oxford and pale blue silk for Cambridge. The dark blue caught my eye, and so Father bought an Oxford doll for each of us, which we then pinned on our lapels. That year was the first of many when Cambridge won, and I was so disappointed that I almost cried in sympathy for 'our' team. Turning to Father for comfort, I saw that his dark blue doll had very deftly been replaced by a pale blue one.

I stared in disbelief, and can say in all honesty that, at that very moment, an important part of my character was formed. I understood in a flash the meaning of hypocrisy and empty pride, and at the age of eight my respect and admiration for Father evaporated, never to return. I do not know why, but this small and seemingly trivial incident has returned to my memory time and time again, as fresh as if the incident took place only yesterday.

*

By now Father had been recommended a school south of the river, and so he found some rooms nearby in Honor Oak. I started my schooling at the age of eight, without a word of English and with a built-in panic of people. 'Oldfield: The House of Education' was a private establishment run by the Misses Pound, three Edwardian spinster sisters, and it was a perfect time warp, like something out of a Joyce Grenfell revue. What had once been their family home was now a large school, the only architectural concession being the conversion of the large conservatory into a gymnasium. All three sisters wore floor-length, high-necked dresses of black or grey, with all sorts of paraphernalia hanging around the neck and waist – chains, watches, spectacles, lorgnettes, scissors ... you name it, they had it! But none of them possessed any teaching qualifications whatsoever, and this also applied to the additional teaching staff employed.

The eldest Miss Pound, the headmistress, was the only erudite one, her single passion being Greek mythology. She duly applied this to everything. She was immensely obese and used to sail into the main schoolroom for morning prayers with her tray of papers, inkstands and pens neatly balanced on her enormous bosom, her arms free to propel her body along like oars. At one particular school function in a local hall she arrived last, as the senior person, and when she sat down, the chair disintegrated very publicly under her enormous bulk. She landed with a crash on the floor, her legs in the air and her skirts swishing, and everybody screamed with laughter. Everybody except me, that is: I burst into tears, for Miss Pound's was the most bitterly poignant humiliation I ever wished to see.

The second sister, Miss Alice, was what would today be termed a real nutter. I even remember her sitting and trimming her toenails while we sat and pondered the mysteries of arithmetic and algebra, or whatever went under that title (she had long ago given up the real thing, if indeed she had ever taken it up – which I doubt). Finally there was Miss Hilda, the youngest sister, who provided the comic relief by continually poking and tweaking us where it most tickled or hurt!

All three sisters looked as if the clothes they wore had been stitched onto them, and that they had worn them forever. Was this only because it seemed inconceivable to envisage them without any? They were the sisters of John Pound, the owner of some superb leather goods shops in the West End – I still remember them in Bond Street and Regent Street long after I left school. John Pound was also Lord Mayor of London twice over, or so the legend went.

The Misses Pound were assisted by a junior mistress who had the extraordinary habit of holding a book with her thumb inserted between the pages and then hitting children on the head with it if they did anything 'wrong' – she would remove her thumb at the last moment so that the book slammed shut as it hit the unfortunate head. There was also a German Fräulein who was so thin and straight that she resembled a figure from a Lowry painting. She suffered from a skin disease and left flakes of dust wherever she went.

This Fräulein was the headmistress's companion, and on a certain day of the week a hansom cab would collect them to go shopping in Forest Hill or Sydenham. However, their expeditions were always undertaken furtively in case anyone should see the immense Miss Pound struggling to squeeze in or out of the cab – she was wider than its door. On one occasion when I had stayed late at school, perhaps to attend Brownies, I happened to see the cab returning from its shopping trip. Miss Pound created the most hilarious picture as she attempted to extricate herself from the cab, her efforts causing it to rock violently, while the German stick insect tried to push her out. When eventually Miss Pound was ejected, it was like a champagne cork popping.

Being a foreigner so soon after World War One was dicey, because to the average suburban child 'foreign' meant 'German' – and thus guilty of everything and anything. So whenever a child at school lost or broke something, the finger of blame was pointed at me. The word 'thief' became a familiar sound to my ears. This, I suppose, was when I developed my non-retaliatory attitude, which has remained with me all my life. I have always believed in my mother's philosophy of '*Qui excuse s'accuse*', and for this I paid harshly. My punishments for the wrongdoings of others became more severe and unjust, and I ended up spending the major part of school lessons either outside in the corridor or in the loo reading *Girl's Own*. This was the teachers' idea of punishment, and no 'research' or 'inquests' were ever bothered with.

As I grew older I found it hard to understand why my father, a highly intelligent man, could allow his daughters to be educated under such appalling conditions. Yet it was easier for my sister Maya: she already had a smattering of education, including English, and had a far more assertive and aggressive nature than I.

And I suppose one should not blame Father too much, since our perpetual financial problems may have meant that school fees were in arrears from time to time, and that a move was therefore impossible. When the American stock market crashed in 1929 and Father's bank went bankrupt, our financial situation became worse than ever.

I eventually finished my formal education at the age of fifteen, by which time the school was slowly but surely choking to death. By a fluke, I came out with an excellent understanding of English and a reasonable degree of general knowledge. But none of my talents as such had been either discussed or nurtured – as was the norm in many other schools of that time. After leaving school I took a shorthand and typing course which, although I was not to use it at the time, would come in very useful many years later.

Mother, who had been ailing for many years, did what she could to give me love and understanding, and she became the pivot of my life. Father had always wanted sons, women being inferior creatures as far as he was concerned, so I had little encouragement from him in my many talents which were waiting to be tapped and which developed still further in later years. I could sing, paint, sew and cook, and I suppose he saw my getting married as the obvious solution to everything.

Had life been kinder to him, Father would have been a delightful man. He was extremely knowledgeable, a gifted sportsman, and talented with his hands. His great love was wood, and he made superb furniture, some of it lovingly carved – even with my initials. But he was a disappointed man, taciturn and afraid of appearing weak by showing any love. He therefore gave little warmth or affection to his children, and even less towards Mother. He withdrew, and remained an enigmatic character for the rest of his life.

4

Prophecy and Faith

WHEN I WAS A TEENAGER, spiritualism was a widespread source of wonder, awe and amusement. My contemporaries and I would gather together and do table-tapping – one knock for 'yes', two knocks for 'no' – to questions asked with bated breath. And it worked. The table (one that had to have been simply glued, rather than nailed, together) would bang out 'yes' or 'no', and I am not joking when I say that it would take off and fly round the ceiling like a mad thing, neither touched nor held by human hand. It would then dodderingly settle itself down in its appointed place, no doubt exhilarated by its flight of freedom.

On one occasion I asked it a slightly disrespectful question and received three very nasty jabs on the tender part of my knee. It was very angry, and I decided that enough was enough – I would now either take it seriously or leave it in peace. However, a friend suggested going to a church service followed by a seance, and I went with her, giggling with anticipation of something weird and wonderful. The medium slowly went into a trance and started pointing at different people, giving messages both personal and impersonal which were obviously meaningful to those concerned. When her finger pointed at me, I stiffened.

Her message started with a little girl of eight, dropping forget-me-nots over my left shoulder. (Here I must remind readers that my half-sister, Vera, died from leukaemia at that age.) Then the medium said to me, 'You will be an opera singer.' This, of course, negated everything else that she had just said. For what did I have to do with being an opera singer? Nothing, but nothing, could then have been further away from me and my circumstances. My friend and I giggled and decided that our interest was over. It was all too ridiculous.

✳

When I was growing up, my mother became involved in Christian Science, and somehow I was able to relate to it myself in quite an important way. I practised its formula of 'mind over matter' on many occasions. In fact I still use one of its jingles as a mantra when stressed or distressed, and it very often works. However, in 1932 a tragedy befell my beloved half-sister Alice in Moscow. While giving birth to a baby boy in hospital she contracted scarlet fever and was moved, without him, to a fever hospital. When she eventually returned to collect him she discovered that he had been allowed to die of starvation. Although we had sent as much dried baby food as we could to the hospital, it had been misappropriated by the authorities.

No religious belief could diminish my own anguish, and my faith was now shattered. Furthermore, something within me died when I saw the Christian Science 'practitioners' – often very wealthy ladies of leisure – charging astronomical fees for their dubious prayers when someone was injured or in trouble. In any case, the Orthodox and Catholic religions had always left me cold.

Although I am now an agnostic, I have dabbled in various beliefs and religions. I believe faith is within us, and that we should be self-sufficient without a 'God' to whom we are subservient; we should find our own church within ourselves and not rely on a man of the cloth to do our thinking for us. However, I feel very strongly that much of the Bible, particularly txhe Ten Commandments, has a great deal to offer us in the way of guidance, provided that we treat it as a philosophy rather than as a handbook of religious belief.

5

Discovery

AT THE AGE OF SIXTEEN I started going to a rather dreary
club in Barons Court, West Kensington, for Russian youngsters. It was there, during our singsongs, that I first discovered I
had a voice. Someone suggested my singing in the Orthodox
Church choir, and so every Sunday I would travel to Victoria where
the church was then situated. But from the start I realized that I
was a threat to the two middle-aged songsters who were fixtures in
the choir. They did all they could to make my visits as unpleasant
as possible, even holding the music out of my range of sight. A
little disheartened, I gave up. But I realize now that it must have
been in the choir that I developed my musical ear and instinct –
the ability to pick up music and retain it.

In 1934, when I was eighteen, a short-lived competition for ama-
teur singers was launched. Called 'the Golden Voice Girl of Great
Britain', it started in South London, and I won every heat in which
I took part. Soon after winning the South London heat in Clapham,
I received a telephone call from a gentleman who introduced him-
self as a representative of Chappells, the music publishers in Bond
Street. It appeared that they had quite a stake in the competition,
for the man asked me whether I would like to win it.

After some hesitation I replied, 'Yes, perhaps I would.' He said,
'Could we meet for lunch and discuss the matter? Would you think
about it and ring me back?' Father was furious when I told him,
and forbade me to accept the invitation – much to my relief, for I
would have been totally unqualified to deal with such a situation.
After that, however, I stopped winning any more heats. All I had to
show for my efforts was a silver cup engraved with the words
'Golden Voice Girl of South London', and I later stupidly threw this
away along with most of my other memorabilia.

Around 1935 Father was fortunate to land a job as an accountant
with a film company, John Stafford Productions. This opened up a
new world to me: it gave me the opportunity of being an 'extra' in
crowd scenes, and provided my first taste of showbiz. I also made
my first theatrical contacts when learning about auditions, agents
and so on. By 1937, and thanks to my initiative, we had moved to
West Kensington. But Father, a deeply unhappy man, kept leaving

us and coming back again, making life very untidy and difficult.

Not being British-born, I was not entitled to any academic scholarships, and there was no way Father could pay for me to go to any college or academy. In fact, when I was nineteen he said to me, 'From now on, you're on your own.' But the die was now cast, there was no going back, and so I soon set out to discover what chances were open to me. The first ever contract that I signed was in 1937 as one of eight showgirls, whatever that term implied, in a second-rate revue called *Sanctions*. The comic lead was played by Ernie Lotinga, a member of the then extremely well-known theatrical family that included Lupino Lane, Stanley Lupino and Ida Lupino.

The main attraction of the show was Phyllis Dixey, the first public stripper of that time. She was very pretty and looked nothing like a stripper, having a rather genteel disposition and appearance, with wonderful platinum blonde hair and huge, innocent-looking blue eyes. During her act she remained incredibly pristine while slowly and coquettishly removing her clothes, piece by piece. At the last moment two enormous ostrich feathers would appear from nowhere, and she would waft them forwards, backwards and then forwards again, concealing the Body Beautiful most successfully from avid eyes.

Ernie Lotinga had an extremely unattractive and untalented brother, Fred, who acted as his sidekick. He was all of five feet tall, and pushy with it. Every Monday, after we had arrived in a new town, the gals of the company would wend their way to the local Woolworth's – a heavenly haven of every necessary and unnecessary girlish requisite, all of them costing under sixpence each. In fact there was nothing for sale in Woolworth's that cost more than sixpence. Somehow or other, Fred would always be lurking in the vicinity, a predator stalking his victims. Picking out his 'taste of the week', he would follow her into the shop and, making a sweeping gesture with his arms, offer the lady of his dreams anything she desired – as long as it cost no more than sixpence. His munificence was breathtaking. He even tried this weekly passion on *me* – but only once.

While on tour in *Sanctions* my immediate plan was to scrape together enough cash to take Mother away for a week. I could not remember her ever having had a holiday or having been on any outings at all, and when Father bought a car – admittedly a tiny Austin Seven – it was for his own exclusive use. I am sure that Mother never rode in it; I certainly did so only rarely, and even then I felt I was trespassing on his territory. Mother came to stay with me while the company was in Derby, and our time together was blissful. I was able to spoil her as much as was possible under the circumstances.

I had intended to take Mother, at the end of that week, to a nice restaurant – an enormous luxury for us both. But before setting out I looked in my purse to make sure that I had the five pound note I had been saving and saw, to my bitter disappointment, that it had vanished. All searches proved futile, and so my dream of dining out together went unfulfilled. Only after Mother had returned to London, and I had landed my next part in a show, did I find the five pound note hiding in the lining of my handbag.

Not long afterwards I became a member of the Chauve-Souris, a superb Russian revue, world-famous for its imagination and sharp wit, while it was on tour from Paris. The history of this revue goes back to St Petersburg in the early 1900s, where Baliev founded the club in a basement where a number of bats had made their home – hence the revue's name. The show included skits on opera, and here again, I instinctively picked up miming and timing that proved invaluable. (I learned recently that the Chauve-Souris has been revived, and is alive and kicking in St Petersburg.)

6

The Bracelet

S EEING AGAIN the portrait photograph of me that was taken around 1937, and which has been reproduced in this book, opens up for me a small and private world of long ago. The bracelet seen in the photograph was a very special gift from a very special person who was extremely kind to me: Princess Andrew of Russia, daughter-in-law of Grand Duchess Xenia.

The Princess had a grace and favour house, adjoining Hampton Court Palace, called Wilderness House. At the bottom of its long garden was a huge garage, and in the rambling flat above lived her son, Prince Andrew, and his wife and family: Betty Frederici, from the Princess's first marriage, exquisitely pretty; Michael, also known as Babka, a dark, strikingly good-looking young man just reaching adulthood; Andrew, also known as Andriousha, a stunningly handsome blond man in his late teens; and Xenia, also known as Mishkin (Russian for little mouse) because of her shy, self-effacing manner – also a stunner, if she had but known it.

My sister Maya had by this time completed her medical training, and she joined this wonderful family as a private nurse to the Princess who, alas, had cancer. Maya and I gelled with the children from the start, being their approximate contemporaries; they were very unspoilt and laid-back, with no sense of self-importance whatsoever. We spent many happy hours and days together, walking by the river and visiting the local fair, and on several other occasions they came to stay at the West London flat in which I am living now. In fact they were like siblings – or at least close cousins – to us. Sadly, the Princess died just before the outbreak of war.

Some time later Prince Andrew married Nadine McDougall, daughter of the flour magnate, and their wedding in Sussex was a very memorable occasion. I caught a train from Victoria that was specially laid on for the Russian contingent, and before long confusion was reigning between 'hers' and 'his' – the landed gentry and the slightly bizarre Ruskies! I vividly remember the two Matveiev sisters – famous for their culinary skills – weighed down with a huge container of their cabbage 'piroshkis' (patties) in case starvation stared them in the face in the wilds of Sussex. Delicious they were, too.

At the beginning of the war Michael became an aeronautical engineer in the Fleet Air Arm. Andrew joined the Navy as an able seaman under Admiral Sir Cecil Harcourt and was involved in many convoys to Murmansk, often acting as a Russian interpreter. On one of these trips he met an old, pre-Revolutionary 'bosun' who was so moved to come face to face with a Romanov that he gave Andrew his most precious possession: a portrait of his own daughter. During this period I was on tour almost all the time, but Andrew used to turn up, like a ray of sunshine, no matter where I was. He even appeared unexpectedly when I was in California in 1948.

Xenia married a GI and went with him to Germany; but the marriage foundered, and some time later she married a Geoffrey Tooth. For some years they lived in Gloucester Square, and one day the local police rang them to ask if they had lost a budgie – they had just rescued one which kept repeating, 'My name is Tooth, and I live in Gloucester Square.' After receiving a negative reply the police rang all the local 'Teeth' listed in the telephone directory, including Tooth the Auctioneers, who offered to give the budgie a home. By that time, however, a policewoman had adopted it!

*

Throughout my youth I steered clear of other Russian émigrés in London because of their insufferable snobbishness and need to out-do each other in their aristocratic credentials. I can illustrate this with a recent example. When an émigré whom I have known since my teens rang me recently, and the conversation turned to the subject of snobbism, I asked, 'But what have *you* to be snobbish about?' Her reply was simple: 'Everything and everybody.' 'Strange', I told her. 'It's the one thing that I cannot *abide*. I am the complete opposite of you.' Her reply was, 'And what do *you* know about snobbery? You came after the Revolution – you are a Soviet Russian.' This attitude has long been familiar to me, and it explains why I was so touched to discover that the *real* Russian aristocrats had extraordinary simplicity and lack of pretentiousness. Andrew and Xenia, with their total self-effacement, exemplified this perfectly.

When Maya was dying in 1967 Xenia kept vigil with me at her bedside – a debt of gratitude, lovingly returned, for Maya's care of her mother nearly thirty years earlier. Soon afterwards she and Geoffrey went to live in a fourteenth-century hunting lodge in the Dordogne, and there Mishkin found joy and peace of mind, surrounded by nature in all its beauty. I stayed with them there, and had a blissful time. Alas, our contact is now rare; we are the same age and live on our memories. I often begged her to visit Russia – having been born in Paris, she had never been to her native country – but she always refused. However, only last year she finally made the trip in order to attend the funeral of her royal relatives, and she saw St Petersburg in all its glory. For the first time, she was herself treated like royalty.

7

Vocal Training

IN 1938 I was engaged to take part in my first BBC broadcast, singing in Teddy Joyce's famous girls' choir. Just as we were about to go on air, I received a phone call telling me that Mother was dying. I rushed home immediately, and within minutes she was gone. She had been tortured by cancer for many years – in those days it often went undiagnosed, and while it was gradually eating into her she was treated for just about everything else instead. She died a shadow of herself, in great suffering and morphined to the hilt, at the age of sixty-three. I was devastated beyond words, but as I had lived with the spectre of her death right from my childhood, it was almost a terrifying relief when it became a reality. Now I no longer had to face the loss of her in my imagination; it had happened, and therefore could never happen again.

However, there was no harmony among the three of us who were left. Father lived his own life, while Maya – a fully-fledged nurse – lived hers. I did the same, or at least I tried to. I knew that I had to sing, whatever happened, but in terms of a vocal career, I had no sense of direction.

While working as a film extra I heard of a voice teacher named Horatio Davies and began to have a weekly lesson with him. I have a vague memory of doing vocal exercises and singing a few popular songs for him, and can remember being most surprised when, at the end of two months, he informed me that he had nothing more to give me because he had taught me all he could. I never quite knew whether this was meant as a compliment!

However, there was now no doubt as to the direction my professional life would take, and through the grapevine I heard of the vocal teacher Manlio Di Veroli, who had had a distinguished career as a first class accompanist, playing for great singers such as Battistini. He had an enchanting mews house just off Marble Arch, and I enjoyed enormously my lessons with him there, which included lovely scales and my first taste of operatic arias. His teaching enabled me to make great progress, and I always returned to see him between touring engagements. Among his many pupils was Harry Secombe, who I always felt could have been as great an opera star as he was a comedian.

Between 1937 and 1941 I toured Britain in such shows as *Balalaika*, *Show Boat*, *Hit the Deck* and *Chu Chin Chow* (in which I sang the lead role). How I managed to pay for my singing lessons out of the pittances I earned in those days I cannot begin to understand. A half-hour lesson cost one guinea – the equivalent of about thirty pounds today – and my 'salary' was somewhere between three pounds fifty and four pounds a week. Out of this, one was expected to pay an agent's commission as well as one's digs and clothing – and to try to save a little something for the periods of 'resting'. When I was looking for work in London I would often walk a distance of about five miles from West Kensington to Leicester Square (the hunting ground) in order to save my bus fare. Fortunately the war brought with it the benefit of work with ENSA (Entertainments National Service Association), with which I could often 'stop the gaps'.

After a time I realized that Di Veroli's method differentiated between the vocal registers – emphasizing in particular the chest register, which he separated from the middle register – and that he wanted me to sing accordingly. This meant consciously pushing the voice downwards and creating a definite break. I also soon realized that forcing the lower register in this way was weakening the top of my voice – the biggest danger for any singer, but particularly for a soprano! Since Di Veroli was adamant about his method of training, there was no way that I could prevent these problems from worsening. By now I understood that although the voice *does* consist of lower, middle and upper registers, it should in fact glide imperceptibly from one register into another.

I therefore had no choice but to part company from Di Veroli and to further my technical studies with Mignon Nevada (the daughter of the great soprano Emma Nevada), whom I had met at the London Musical Club. She taught the Marchesi method and had sung a great deal with the Thomas Beecham Opera Company, but when war broke out in 1939 she gave up singing and worked for the Foreign Office, mostly in Bermuda. She was in her fifties when I met her, and although her voice had virtually disappeared and she had difficulty keeping in pitch, she gave me what I needed: a completely unbroken vocal line over more than two and a half octaves, smooth and evenly flowing in one perfect sweep. By this time I was already fairly experienced as a singer, and – as always – my instinct boosted my technique, which must have been pretty solid, as it has lasted into my eighties.

✳

When I went to Italy in the mid-1950s and worked there for long periods, I had the good fortune to come across Mario Ricci, a superb co-repetiteur who simply inspired singers to sing well. He gave me confidence, and helped me with interpretation and classical *portamenti* and *legati*. Much later, the trauma of living through my impresario-manager's death and its aftermath made me feel as though my voice had somehow died within me, but through a close friend I met the wonderful Peter Uppcher, a light operetta singer who had performed with the likes of Evelyn Laye. He had a superb technique that he passed on to me most generously, and which I was able to put to spectacular use every time a singing engagement came along to interrupt my secretarial career. In fact this technique was so foolproof that my voice seemed infallible: it was simply there whenever I picked it up again. Peter's have been my most beloved vocal exercises – so joyous and so rewarding to sing – and when he died, a superb and underrated maestro died with him.

✳

In recent years I myself have dipped into teaching, but for some reason it brings me little satisfaction. To me, singing is entirely natural – so logical and simple – and I find this hard to impart to aspiring vocalists. Most have either been brainwashed into believing that singing is a very physically exacting occupation, and are therefore astonished by the simplicity that I put before them, or they are unable to allow their voices to float on a pure 'line' of breath that involves no muscular exertion. They usually joke, 'You were *born* with your voice, so don't expect the same from me!' I also find that singers try to listen to the sounds they make, but as far as I am concerned, this is taboo. One judges one's own singing not by the sound in the ears but by the sensation in the 'mask' (the facial cavities around the nose, mouth and sinuses) that the placement of notes creates.

Correct placement is, in fact, crucial to singing, for each note has its own position within the mask. So when a singer is conscious of the correctness of each vocal position, he or she will automatically know, by the sensation produced, that the resulting tone is also the correct one. For example, the higher the note, the higher the breath in the mask. Indeed, I believe that the breath should be thought of as something elastic, and that for high notes one should create in the top of the head the sensation of a cupola of breath within which they reverberate. In fact one must always start a vocal phrase knowing exactly what colour and intensity of tone one intends to give it, so that it flows up or down in a single sweep. This also allows for a filtering diminuendo over which the singer has complete control.

In my vocal technique, no facial muscles are used when singing (one should never sing from a dropped jaw and wide-open mouth) as this merely diverts the sound from its central position in the mask. One can also create a tremendous crescendo by spiralling the breath into the mask, for it is not the loudness of the note but the roundness and intensity of tone that count. When this method is perfected, the voice can project across the loudest orchestra and reach the furthest corners of any auditorium. And because the vocal chords and facial muscles are not being used to *project* the sound, one can sing without fear of strain or fatigue.

Correct physical stance is also very important when performing on the concert platform or operatic stage. I always advocate that a singer should stand on the balls of the feet, as this gives both elegance and elasticity, drawing up the figure ready for any potential movement. I also believe that arm and hand movements, if appropriate, should always start on a curved (circular or semicircular) line rather than projecting straight out from the body.

8

Vic Oliver

WHEN WAR BROKE OUT IN 1939, Vic Oliver, the famous Austrian comedian and brilliant – but as yet unfulfilled – musician, was the head of German propaganda for the BBC. He was looking for German-speaking singers to fill out his programmes, and an agent sent me to him for an audition. I sang some Schubert in German. He was interested but not smitten, and asked me what else I sang. When I replied that I also specialized in Russian gypsy songs, his face lit up with excitement and he urged me to let him hear something from this repertoire. By a stroke of luck, Egon Stein, the accompanist I had brought with me, had recently made a superb arrangement of two wonderful Russian gypsy songs, interweaving their melodies into a sensational number, and so he was able to play this with me from memory. Vic was bowled over and said, 'To hell with German Lieder, you are going to top the Variety Bill with me on my next tour.'

The Variety circuit was under the management of Moss Empires, and Vic made a date for me to call at their office to discuss my contract. I was told that this involved having my own, quite costly, orchestral arrangements, my own stage costume (also costly), and accommodation in top class hotels on tour. For this I was offered a salary of fifteen pounds a week – a mere pittance, even then, for someone 'starring' in Variety.

When I showed my amazement and inferred that I could in no way accept so small a salary, I was told that this was the sum nominated to me, and that if I were not satisfied I was to discuss it with Vic. On approaching him, he replied that the matter was nothing to do with him and that I must continue negotiations with Moss Empires. For several weeks I was therefore 'ping-ponged' between Vic and Moss Empires.

Vic also told me, in no uncertain terms, that there was a long queue of well-known singers willing to pay a large sum for the privilege of starring with him. By this time, word had gone round the theatre world that I was going to 'star' with Vic Oliver, and so my position became rather embarrassing. Had I slipped out of the contract, my career could have come to a sticky end, so I had no choice but to sign and put on as good a face as I could.

Vic's argument was that my star position on the Variety billings was worth, *status-wise*, at least a hundred pounds per week to anyone in the know, and that I had to accept this fact. Only he, I, and the Moss organization knew the actual sum I was receiving. Having yoyo-ed between the Moss group and Vic until the very last moment, I found out that he himself was actually the boss of the organization, holding fifty-one percent of its shares, and that my salary was therefore entirely *his* decision.

Vic's first wife had been a concert singer and he was her accompanist in concert and music halls in the USA. While performing at one of these theatres Vic sat down on his piano stool and it promptly broke under his weight. The audience, thinking this was part of the act, screamed with laughter and applauded wildly. And so Vic Oliver the comedian was born (his real name, incidentally, was Baron Samek). Like many comedians, he had no sense of humour whatsoever, especially against himself. In fact, he was one of the most ambivalent and devious characters I was ever to meet.

The moment he was sure that you were at ease with him and basking in his *bonhomie*, his attitude could, and did, change in a flash. From a warm, friendly, delightful person, he would instantly change into icy formality, dismissing you and leaving you totally shocked and humiliated. When I appeared with him in Variety and was, by his standards, over-enthusiastically received (this often happened), I would be 'in Coventry' for a long period of time. From time to time he would terminate my contract, telling me that I was no longer needed and that I was to leave at the end of the week. But later, when his anger had cooled, he would beg me to return.

When staying in the same hotels as he and his coterie, I would enter the dining-room after the show and be shown to a single table. No sooner had I sat down than he would beckon a waiter and point meaningfully at me. The waiter would then come in my direction, bow deferentially, and request me, on behalf of Mr Oliver, to join his table. The following day the waiter, taking this as a logical pattern to follow, would show me to Vic's table, only to be told peremptorily that I was to have a table to myself. After a while I did my best to accommodate myself in a different hotel to his, in order to save myself unnecessary embarrassment.

If Vic knew that I would be rushing to catch the last evening train home to London after a Saturday performance, he would deliberately lengthen his act to make sure I would miss it, all the while ironically looking first at his watch and then in my direction where I was waiting in the wings for him to finish. Many was the time that I was left with no option but to take the night train, arriving in London sleepless and exhausted. I would get home just in time to have a quick breakfast and to spruce myself up for a morning rehearsal of *Vic Oliver Introduces*, a weekly BBC radio programme recorded at the People's Palace in Mile End Road. Vic would then be charm itself, warm and affectionate. He himself needed only five hours' sleep a day, and travelled everywhere by car.

He had a habit of adopting young girls from a reasonably humble background and grooming them into tweedy 'Sloane Ranger' types with only a touch of makeup and a pretentious Oxbridge accent. They nevertheless had to have some sort of talent to be part of his stage ensemble. One of them was June Manton, a very pretty ex-Cockney girl with a slight singing voice. Vic dreamed up a sketch tailored to her looks and talent: he would sit at the piano, play a medley of semi-classical music, and then *segue*, through changing chords, into Schubert's Ave Maria. At that moment, a light behind him would illuminate a black, veil-like curtain through which could be seen the silhouetted profile of a nun in a praying position, singing this well-known prayer.

After some weeks Vic dismissed June from this sketch, for reasons known only to himself, and used me instead. I enjoyed the experience, except for the fact that, as always, Vic delighted in making me suffer. He succeeded in doing this by testing me, leading up to the Ave Maria melody and then suddenly changing course to play something totally unexpected. He knew full well, of course, that I had already taken a deep breath and opened my mouth ready for the first notes. This little comedy could sometimes go on for several minutes until my nerves were at breaking point. All I can hope is that it enriched *his* life!

Alongside his gift for comedy, Vic was genuinely a brilliant musician, and after a time, his love of music nudged him into forming his own orchestra, the British Symphony. I was his first soloist, and at this point I must say that, notwithstanding all his cruel jokes and dirty tricks, he and he alone really evaluated my voice. It was he who allowed me to use it to its full potential by singing the great operatic arias that had lain dormant for quite a few years, there having been a hiatus of great singers in Britain after the 1930s. But again, if my success as a soloist was too great for his liking, I was punished!

On some occasions it was me – with the backing of Vic's orchestra – that hall managers were particularly keen to rebook. Vic resented the fact that such bookings depended on my availability as much as on his, and he would therefore claim that I would not be available on the dates in question because I was already engaged to sing somewhere else. I never managed to avoid this by discovering the recipe for singing well but not *so* well as to generate as much spontaneous applause as I usually received. *Is* there such a recipe? In any case, Vic knew better than anyone if I was below par vocally, and he would never have tolerated an even slightly sub-standard performance.

It was well known in showbusiness circles that Vic's 'personal entertainment' involved some rather bizarre practices. I was therefore relieved to learn that he considered me, at twenty-five, far too old to be involved in his private pastimes. However, he once told me most vehemently that there was no way that one could remain normal – physically or morally – while making a career in showbusiness, and he advised me to do something about it as soon as possible, or else!

Although most of the music I sang with Vic was classical and brought me huge success, mainly with the BBC, my artistic status was suspect because of my association with his name and, I suppose, his reputation as a comedian. But I do know how many established operatic singers would have given their eye-teeth to be on his programme. As proof of this, when I later started to travel abroad or was otherwise unavailable for engagements with him, he was able to fill my place with the best singers in the land. The 'stigma' was by then shrinking, and he would often mention a well-known singer to me and remark, 'I gave her the *Ernani* aria to sing, but, as always, no one can do it as well as you can. Why?'

I have often wondered why a man who made such a huge career in so many fields, and whose name was synonymous with 'Mr Showbiz', should subsequently have been forgotten. One never hears him mentioned now, nostalgically or otherwise. When he died in the early 1960s, I was asked to sing 'Jesu, Child of My Rejoicing' at his memorial service, but this would have involved rehearsing with an orchestra; and as I was then bashing away on a typewriter at the BBC, I was unable to take the time off, much to my regret. However, I did manage to sneak out for the service itself, at the Artist's Church in Holborn, and remembered vividly the undeniable charm and warmth of this man.

A postscript: Vic Oliver was also an actor, and went to South

9

The London Musical Club

JOSEPH SAXBY was a very well-known pianist/harpsichordist in the late 1930s and early 1940s, and he acted as my accompanist whenever he could. At that time he was staying at the London Musical Club, not far from my home in West Kensington. One morning we had arranged to rehearse together at my flat, and when the bell rang and I opened the door, I was surprised to see not Joseph but a slightly eccentric-looking middle-aged lady. Noticing my expression, she quickly explained that Joseph had had a sudden change of plan and that, so as not to let me down, she had come in his place.

From that moment on, Adela Hamaton (also known by her married name of Adela Armstrong) became an integral part of my life. She was the owner of the London Musical Club, and invited me to visit it whenever I was free. She also offered to act as my accompanist whenever I needed one, and so, from about 1939 to 1962, the club became my second home whenever I was in London. It was situated in a superb Victorian semi-detached mansion in Holland Park. Its atmosphere was always relaxed, warm and welcoming, and Mrs A, as she was lovingly called, seemed unruffled in the midst of what was actually permanent chaos.

Although the place was seething with music students of all ages and callings, by some fluke the splendid Music Room with its three grand pianos was almost always free when I needed to practice – as was my beloved Mrs A. We would spend hours working together, I learning an ever-growing repertoire and she accompanying me to her heart's content. I do not remember ever looking at a clock or worrying about the time; we simply carried on for as long as our energies allowed us. Nor was any money exchanged, and I never felt beholden to her. The work gave her pleasure, and so she indulged herself – and me.

She also accompanied my first Wigmore Hall recital – a joint concert featuring a fine pianist by the name of Boris Ferber in the first half, and me singing in the second half. All I remember of the concert, apart from Mrs A's superb accompaniment of my songs, is that after the interval I had to make my way to the platform against a stampede of Boris's fans. By the time I got there, the hall was half-empty – his audience obviously had no interest in me whatsoever. This was rather disconcerting for a budding recitalist, and an early example to me of professional egoism and arrogance.

At that time, the London Musical Club was the spawning-ground for all aspiring artists. Instrumentalists, vocalists and even a few dancers all mixed freely, though instrumentalists were clearly in the majority. Famous names, as well as those on the brink of success, passed through the club's doors. One of them was Alexis Kligerman, a superb pianist with almost too much potential who, through some difficulty in accepting life as it was, cut short his career while he was at his peak. Another great pianist at the club was Peter Katin, who only recently celebrated his fiftieth year as a recitalist at the Wigmore Hall. Boyd Neel was also a regular visitor.

The club was a notable venue for auditions and trial performances 'before the real thing', and the Music Room could seat an audience of about a hundred. The house itself was in a fairly fragile state of decoration, but such things were unimportant in wartime. I have a vivid memory of walking down the spacious stairs with Mrs A and pausing on a landing just as the ceiling crashed down around us. I managed to avert its falling on me, but poor Mrs A took the brunt of the impact and was covered in plaster, looking like something out of *Blithe Spirit*. There was general panic and much rushing around with shrieks of concern, but Mrs A stood unflustered, shaking her head gently and saying, 'What's all the fuss about? Hasn't anyone ever seen a ceiling collapse before?'

Another evening, during a concert at the club, we suddenly heard the whine of a doodlebug. In a flash, every man in the audience dived under the three grand pianos, only to emerge very shamefacedly once the danger had passed – all the ladies had remained composed and serene in their seats.

One day I arrived with my coach, Maestro Bottino, to find the Music Room engaged, so Mrs A kindly lent me her bedroom which, although in total chaos, contained a piano. My coach, a randy little individual, was expecting a phone call from his girlfriend, and I will never forget the sight of him rummaging for the telephone when it finally rang. There was no sign of it whatsoever, but after it had rung for some time he managed to locate it by crawling on the ground and retrieving it from a pile of God-knowswhat under the enormous double bed.

The London Musical Club was rich with dogs and cats who lived their lives to the same pattern as Mrs A's – always on the brink of some emergency or calamity, yet always unruffled and emanating warmth and camaraderie. Mrs A was the one person who never let me down, even finding a home for my beloved tabby and white cat Tobias when I had to go away. She placed him with some university 'crammers' by the name of Davies and Son whose premises were situated opposite the club; they took him in, made a bed for him in the Director's out-tray, and nominated him an honorary professor (a most apt title for a cat of his erudition). When the time came for me to reclaim him, the entire staff, and particularly the Director himself, mourned his going.

*

A couple of years ago I had the pleasure of meeting Alberto Portugeis, the brilliant Argentine pianist. He lives around the corner from me, so we now see a lot of each other, and he was able to tell me the end of the story of the London Musical Club. Alberto discovered the club when he arrived in London in 1967, and stayed there for quite some time. The atmosphere was apparently as bohemian as ever, and he recalled that Mrs A kept a couple of enormous mastiff dogs that had a litter of pups. The room that Alberto was allocated had been used as the mastiff nursery, and the carpet had borne the full brunt of life in the canine kindergarten. Poor Alberto tried endlessly to have it cleaned, but eventually gave up and bought a new one.

Between us, Alberto and I were able to add quite a few names to the list of 'Greats' who passed through the club's doors. They included Martha Argerich, Richard Arnell, Steven Bishop-Kovacevich, Moura Lympany (who had studied with Adela Hamaton, aka Mrs A), Yan Pascal Tortelier, Jacqueline Du Pré, Fou Ts'ong, Rafael Kozco, Desmond Bradley (First Violin with the New Philharmonia Orchestra), and Julius Katchen – who lived at the club.

When Mrs A died in 1973, Eve Spooner took over the management of the club. But soon afterwards the two buildings that it occupied were sold, and the London Musical Club became, to some very special people, nothing but a wonderful memory.

10

Timothy Lloyd

I CANNOT LEAVE TIMOTHY LLOYD out of this book. Although his life was a short one, he left behind many lovely memories and so much warmth and joy. My own life would have been a far emptier one without him.

We were brought together at the beginning of the war when we were entertaining the troops with ENSA. Timothy was a puppeteer who made his own models and worked them in full view of the audience. His fingers manipulated the strings superbly, and the 'artists' – Marlene Dietrich, Frances Day, Carrol Gibbons and many others – moved to their own recordings. Where this wonderful talent came from is a mystery, but it was certainly quite extraordinary.

Timothy was tall – lanky, one might even say – with gorgeous blue eyes and blond, curly hair. His face was cherubic, but with just enough wickedness to make it interesting and enticing. He came from the landed gentry, and paid dearly for his blue blood by attracting all sorts of insect pests – you name them, they bit him! I was always very smug about this because they steered clear of me – doubtless due to my 'peasant' blood. Despite this, and the fact that at nineteen he was four years younger than I, we gelled at once and became more or less inseparable.

Among the other artists in the ENSA group, Timothy and I stood out like sore thumbs. To begin with, we spoke the King's English – unheard of in the ranks of Variety entertainment in those days. Furthermore, in that bizarre atmosphere at the beginning of the war, and for the only time in my life, I had clout. I cannot explain why, but in those days I spoke up for myself – unbelievably, I was nicknamed the Duchess – and demanded my rights, the most important of which was good accommodation. And I got it – or as near as was available. Timothy soon cottoned on to this and became my unofficial sidekick, so the two of us had the pick of the digs which, in the smaller towns, were still sometimes rather grotty.

On one particular occasion we were near Kettering, not far from where Timothy's family lived, and as usual we were allocated the swishest digs in town. The small sitting-room/dining-room was chock-a-block with unimaginable paraphernalia: plaster ducks flying in every direction, Alsatian dogs straining at leashes held by ceramic ladies with flowing skirts, and so on. In fact there was not an inch of uncluttered space. The food was plentiful and reasonable, but although the butter was served in half-pound slabs it was often imprinted with three black finger-marks – this mystery was eventually solved when we learned that our host was a chimney sweep! On several occasions when I returned after a show, I found that my bed had been used by someone else – and for a purpose other than sleeping – but there was very little I could do about it.

That weekend, Timothy went off to his stately home, where life was untainted by the privations of war. Everyone dressed for dinner, the gents in velvet smoking jackets and the ladies with daring *décolletages* and bare arms. One such rare creature was sitting next to Timothy and discoursing politely when she suddenly started screaming in horror and frantically swiping and swishing with her hands – a bug was sauntering up her delicate white arm. Timothy, the obvious source of this foreign body, was physically removed, stripped of his clothes (which were then fumigated), and thrown into a bath heavy with disinfectant. His disgrace was complete. From then on, his parents' disapproval of his professional contribution to the war effort escalated, and further weekend visits to the family home were less than welcome.

Another evening, Timothy and I must have over-imbibed at the officers' mess, and going home in the blackout I realized that I had to spend a penny there and then. We found a suitable yard in which I could attend this call of nature, but in the process I dropped my handbag, spilling its contents onto the ground among the deep, damp leaves and other debris. Timothy saw what had happened and scrabbled to put back what had fallen out of my bag, unintentionally augmenting this with old bus tickets, bottle tops, and other rubbish that I did not discover until the following day.

Arriving at our digs, we found a cold supper awaiting us. It looked revolting, with a plate of what was obviously horsemeat – then an everyday item on most menus – as the *pièce de résistance*. I remember picking up these slices of meat and flinging them all over the room as a gesture of disgust and protest before being violently sick in the 'jerry' which I had found, just in time, under the bed. Timothy, himself swaying heavily, held my forehead to make the going easier for me; then, seeing me flop into bed, he went off to his own room.

The following morning I felt fine and tiptoed into Timothy's bed-room to wake him. He was fast asleep, enveloped in alcoholic fumes, with his right hand on the coverlet. To my amazement, two of his fingernails were painted scarlet – a mystery that could easily have been misinterpreted. It was solved when he told me that, not wishing to embarrass me while lovingly administering to my needs the previous night, he had quickly grabbed my nail varnish and daubed his nails with it so that I would think it had been my *own* hand holding my head while I was ill! It was a bizarre thing to have done, but the motive was enchanting.

Timothy had attended public school but wanted to break out and face the real world. When the time for his conscription came, he was determined to avoid nepotism and therefore chose to enlist as an ordinary private in the East End of London. He nevertheless ended up as a lieutenant in the Green Howards, and in-between calls of duty his social life was full – he fulfilled the role of deb's delight with great panache. Incidentally, his recipe for staying rela-tively sober was to gulp a cup of olive oil before starting on the booze and between social engagements. This certainly seemed to work, ensuring that he was empty for the next party!

He sometimes stayed with me in London, and often had diffi-culty finding his way in the dense blackout and pea-souper fogs. I therefore devised a plan to help him; as he was approaching my flat he would start whistling the tune to

I l-l-love you so, I n-n-need you so,
I w-w-want to know if you
L-l-l-love me just as m-m-much
As I love you . . .

which had been one of Frances Day's hits that he used in his puppet show and which became our own special song. I would be waiting on the street corner, and as soon as I heard his whistling, I would rush to meet him.

Before long he went off to war, still radiant and so full of life. Whenever he could, he wrote me letters which, though censored, were a joy to receive. As a token of my affection I sent him a silver chain with an identity disc inscribed with his name and number. In 1942 he reached Italy and found himself in the midst of very serious fighting. At that time I was on tour, and coming home one weekend I found in the mail an envelope containing his identity disc and the date of his death. My desolation was beyond words, and I knew that life would never be the same again.

He had been among the armed forces who took Rome for the Allies, and he then went on to Cassino. While there, he heard some soldiers in the distance and challenged them. They shouted back in Italian, 'Friends! Friends! We're Italian!', and so, greatly relieved, he made his way towards them. When he reached them, they shot him at point-blank range. He was only twenty-two. He was buried by the side of the road, where he fell.

Fifty-four years later, in 1996, an article about me appeared in the *Daily Telegraph*, and throughout that day my phone did not stop ringing. People I had known well but not seen for years called me, as did people I had known briefly but meaningfully. Timothy's nephew Sampson also rang me. It took me quite a time to realize who he was, and when I did, I burst into tears. Sampson himself then broke down. It appeared that a biography of Timothy Lloyd, *A Clear Premonition*, had been published the previous year, at about the time that my first CD was released, but somehow this had passed me by. Both Sampson and the biographer, Raleigh Trevelyan, had tried everywhere – all over England and all over the world – to locate me, but they had come up empty-handed. The *Telegraph's* article mentioned that I lived in London, and it gave Sampson the idea of looking for me in the telephone directory, where he found me. I had been so near, and yet so far away.

I was mentioned a number of times in the biography, and the author quoted a rave review of my début in *The Fair of Sorochintsi* that Timothy had attended. The critic's comment was 'This is the Voice of the Year'. But because Raleigh Trevelyan had not been able to contact me while undertaking his research, little more could be said about me. His book was based largely around the letters that Timothy wrote to his beloved mother – gentle, placatory letters to ease her fears and abate her sorrows. The letters that he sent me were vastly different, leaving little to the imagination. The last was dated about two days before his death, and when reading it, one somehow sensed that the end was inevitable. Had Raleigh Trevelyan been able to locate me earlier, the published book would have been vastly different – far more pungent, and showing another side of Timothy.

In 1998, after reading an article about me in the *Sunday Times Magazine's* 'A Life in the Day of...', I received a letter from Mary Fraser-Tytler, an ex-ENSA colleague who had joined us as a violinist for a very short run – and who also spoke the King's English! Now Lady Morgan, and the widow of an admiral who, for some time, had been in charge of the Royal Yacht *Britannia*, she had

11

Other Early Encounters

O NE OF THE MANY ARTISTS I worked with in ENSA was
Nellie Wallace, a great Variety performer of the day and a great
character. We were stationed near Llandudno in a NAAFI hostel,
and one morning, as I came out of my room on the top floor, I
encountered Nellie doing her 'bar-work' exercises. She was hanging
on to the railings with one hand and doing 'lift-ups' in her long-
johns, muttering to herself, 'No. They don't make 'em like us any
more...'

She left us after the first week to join another group, and the
following day the hostel received a telegram explaining that she
had left her Sunday best dentures in a glass by her bed. Could they
please be sent to her at once?

*

At the end of 1941 *Show Boat*, in which I had 'a cough and a spit',
arrived in Glasgow, and we came to a halt there as the first bombs
hit the city at the beginning of the Blitz. All the London theatres
were now closed, and the prospects looked pretty gloomy. (I remember that one day, while we were rehearsing the same production of *Show Boat* at the old Scala Theatre in London prior to the
tour, we came out of the theatre for a break and had to dodge
shrapnel raining down from above and churning up the
pavements.)

Stranded in Glasgow, I was encouraged to audition for the role
of Bonnie Prince Charlie in the pantomime of that name, which
was going to be put on at the historic Metropole Theatre in the
heart of the Gorbals. Unbelievably, I got the part, despite being
Russian – and a Russian 'Sassenach', at that! There were going to
be five pantomimes in Glasgow that Christmas, with Evelyn Laye at
the top at the Alhambra and with me at the bottom at the Met. In
between were Elizabeth French, Elsie Percival, and someone else
whose name escapes me.

The Scottish BBC had the brilliant idea of doing a broadcast that
included all five of us, and which was to be called 'All Boys
Together'. At the rehearsal we sang through our numbers in order
of priority, so I was last. When I finished my 'Afton Waters' Evelyn
Laye applauded vigorously and said, 'This girl has to be given more

to sing. Cut out one of my numbers and give *her* the time.' I have never forgotten this gesture. 'Boo' Laye, as she was known, was the first 'Great' who crossed my conscious path, and what generosity she showed a shy beginner.

In a way Evelyn adopted me, inviting me to her lovely digs in Bath Street, which I also used in later years with great joy. She was a very warm, extrovert person who bubbled over with vitality and humanity. Her mother, whom I also came to know quite well, was even more outrageous, though rather autocratic-looking. Not long ago I reread a lengthy letter that I wrote to my sister Maya during those days; it was full of Evelyn and her mother, and there is a nice little paragraph about the older woman: 'She smoked like a chimney, swore like a trouper, drank like a fish, and looked like Queen Mary.'

I also remember the night that Evelyn's husband, the actor Frank Lawton, was due to arrive on the late train. Boo was very restless and excited, and washed her hair twice during the evening, just for something to do! She made many attempts to further our friendship, but at that time I felt I could not compete with her glamorous and sophisticated lifestyle. It was a world away from mine. Hearing my voice aroused in her a great desire to better her own, which she had sadly allowed to deteriorate, developing a way of singing everything below pitch. I vividly remember her saying, 'Dahling, with my looks and your voice ... can you imagine?'

Another time, I was singing a Russian gypsy song that finished with three forte, staccato top Cs, and I heard Evelyn exclaim, 'Jesus Christ! There you are, singing three top Cs, and I can't even get a bloody G!' She asked her friend John McCormack to recommend a good teacher, and he suggested Dino Borgioli, then recently retired from singing and ready for a second career as a teacher. Through Evelyn, he gathered a large circle of pupils, among them Joan Hammond. One of the last times that I visited Evelyn at her St John's Wood flat, Borgioli was also a guest, and we had a fabulous evening singing every duet possible, just for the sheer joy of it.

That was not my first meeting with Borgioli. Many years earlier, when I was just beginning my career, he placed an advertisement in *The Stage*, inviting singers to audition for him. I went along and sang, and he seemed most enthusiastic about my voice. He invited me to join him on a long trip to his native Italy as his 'pupil', giving 'display' concerts in that capacity. However, as I would have had to pay my own expenses, there was no way that I could afford to accept his offer, much as I would have adored to. But looking back, it seems strange that, however obliquely, I was in some way responsible for his career as a maestro.

But back to *Bonnie Prince Charlie*. After reaching a verbal agreement with the pantomime bosses I returned to London to await the dates of the rehearsals. At that time my stage name was Kyra Vronska, and the management suddenly realized that, being Russian, it could jeopardize the season – Russia was still on Germany's side. They therefore sent me a telegram that read: SUGGEST CHANGE NAME TO VERA KAY – OR CONTRACT VOID. Panic-stricken, I quickly came up with 'Vayne' (anything rather than Vera Kay!) and this was accepted. However, by the time rehearsals began, Russia had joined the UK against Hitler, and so I could have kept 'Vronska' after all!

Yet even this was not the end of the story. By the time I – with my new name – arrived back in Glasgow for the rehearsals, the management had realized with regret that 'Vronska' was actually more Polish than Russian; and since there was a large number of Polish troops in Scotland, they decided to commercialize on it by fabricating newspaper stories, complete with exotic headlines, about my Polish nationality. So, having Anglicized my name, I suddenly became a Pole!

✳

At this point an enchanting person entered my life. I cannot remember how I acquired him, but suddenly, there he was. Andy Duncan, almost too Scottish to be true, my first and last Stage Door Johnny! He was my shadow and soon, willy-nilly, became my minder – for a very good reason. For as long as I can remember, I have somehow been resented by many people, though I will never understand why. I never threw my weight around and I was never envious of what other singers were, or had; I simply did my job and left others to do theirs. But that is not how the cookie seemed to crumble, even in this particular pantomime.

For example, the Bonnie Prince's right-hand man was a good-looking, brawny baritone who, as well as lusting after me, resented *my* being the Prince. In addition, I faced hostility from my Principal girl, Amy, and her sister Ivy. They were a well-known double act on the Scottish Variety stage, and Ivy had been given the small part of a 'confidante' in *Bonnie Prince Charlie* in order that both girls could have a place in the show. From their point of view, they would have made the perfect Prince Charlie and his lady-love, so they, too, resented me. Fortunately my minder was there to keep all enemies at bay.

I had been warned before the pantomime opened that if the audience did not like a performer, they would be quick to show their disapproval. This usually took the form of rotten eggs, over-ripe tomatoes, and in fact anything gungy and smelly, being ex-pertly aimed at the offender in question. I felt totally vulnerable on all fronts, without even nationalistic qualifications for playing their beloved hero, and I therefore had enormous qualms. But, to my immense relief, the first night of the pantomime was a huge suc-cess, and when I left the stage door I was dazzled by two rows of immaculate Polish officers waiting to salute their 'countrywoman'.

They stormed me, clicked their heels, kissed my hand, and screamed at me in Polish. All I could do was to keep repeating, more and more desperately, 'Excuse me, I am Russian and do not speak Polish.' When my words suddenly sank in, the Polish contin-gent vanished in a flash – all except for one brave warrior who asked for the pleasure of my company. But Andy came too, and somehow we did not work as a trio!

Andy Duncan was a supplies manager for the merchant navy (stationed locally) at the large outfitters, Paisleys of Buchanan Street, and so, I suppose, he had contacts and perks. During re-hearsals, and without a word to me, he took the measurements of my rather grotty dressing room, and by the first night every wall had been covered in a lovely cretonne material, perfectly tailored to size, with pockets for all my personal effects. He also fitted me out in the most superb Royal Stewart kilts with all the relevant paraphernalia.

As we settled into the run of performances at the Met my panic left me, and I began to feel quite secure. Then one day all hell was let loose in the middle of my solo 'When you wish upon a star'. The theatre became wild with whistling, stamping and catcalls, and I steeled myself for the sludgy onslaught. But as the noise and stamping continued, I realized that the commotion was focused on something near my feet. I looked down cautiously and saw a gor-geous cat sitting there, washing itself contentedly. It had obviously got its pantomime venues confused, ending up with 'Charlie' in-stead of 'Dick'. I picked it up, carried it off the stage, and continued the song where I had left off.

Andy kept watch outside my door at every performance, and presented me, nightly, with a half bottle of gin and a half bottle of lime – my innocuous tipple at the time. Somehow, out of a sense of gratitude and a desire not to offend him, I managed to work my way through these refreshments nightly! Thank God, the pantomime eventually ended its run and I was able to kick the habit – I had already found it hard to perform without this stimulant. Andy himself was an alcoholic, and in all the months I knew him, I never saw him even slightly sober. In fact this, to me, was the *real* Andy. After a quick gulp of water first thing in the morning he was well away again, yet he managed to function beautifully at both work and play.

Every Thursday, when Paisleys had a half-day, Andy would take me for lunch at Roganos, then one of the finest restaurants in town, where I could indulge in anything I wanted. Then we would go off to the cinema where, the moment he sat down, he fell fast asleep, snoring gently as a contented background to the movie. He would wake just as the titles came up. I myself started to imbibe on Sundays, doubtless to keep Andy company, but at that time one could not buy alcohol on Sundays unless one was a bona fide traveller from outside Glasgow – one had to sign the hotel register stating that one was travelling from A to C via B and had broken the journey for refreshment. Needless to say, Andy managed to find a way round this obstacle and always seemed to have a couple of train or coach tickets as 'open sesames' to our favourite hotel bar.

On the way home in the blackout, I developed a penchant for ringing the doorbells of any imposing houses we passed and then sprinting out of sight. To light our way, Andy had provided me with a torch, and on one particular evening I was using it as a guide to stealthily approach an expensive-looking door decorated with brass knockers and bells. I was suddenly met by the light of another stealthily approaching torch, and working my beam upwards to peer at the face of its owner, I was stunned to see a policeman gazing quizzically at me and trying to conceal a smile. The two of us burst out laughing and shook hands, and after I had listened intently to his gentle admonition, we went our separate ways.

When, on the occasion of my twenty-sixth birthday, my sister Maya sent Andy some cash to buy me a handbag, he presented me with a huge bouquet of flowers that concealed a black antelope handbag with a gold chain. It was of such exquisite beauty that I burst into a paroxysm of tears at the sight of it. How much extra he must have forked out I cannot imagine, but it must have been a small fortune.

I do not think I ever had a conversation, as such, with my darling Andy; we seemed to have a mental language that was very rich and quite sufficient. He never, ever so much as touched me, for he had far too much loyalty and respect for me. He also had a wife and family, but they were never mentioned. Nor did I ever ask questions about them; it was understood that they were part of his other life. I have only one photo of Andy, dressed up in his beloved drum major's outfit with huge bearskin hat, drum and sticks at the ready, listing heavily to one side, eyes glazed and completely crossed – one puff of wind and he would have keeled over!

Many years later, long after I left Glasgow, Andy would suddenly appear on my doorstep in London, as sloshed and ebullient as ever. We would have a drink together and think of the old times. I never had his address, however, so there was no correspondence between us. In the end he disappeared from my life as unobtrusively as he had walked into it, leaving a gap never to be filled.

12

The Clippie and the Sunday Coat

ALTHOUGH I CANNOT explain why, I love Glasgow and often return to it in my mind. It was always autumn or winter when I was there, and the weather was always diabolical – misty or foggy, with a perpetual oily, clinging drizzle. But this somehow made the place seem so personal, and many of my memories of the city are funny ones.

While I was in Glasgow for *Bonnie Prince Charlie* I witnessed two innovations: the birth of the 'Clippie' for the tramcars that criss-crossed the city, and the influx of city gents from the Foreign Office in London who had been sent to Glasgow for safety, well away from the firing line. One would often see these urban hybrids sauntering down Sauchiehall Street, resplendent in their uniform of black jacket, striped trousers, bowler hat, umbrella in the right hand, and portfolio and copy of *The Times* in the left.

One day one of these gentlemen jumped onto a tramcar, smiling blithely, and, raising his hat politely, asked if there were any seats upstairs. The clippie looked him up and down slowly and disdainfully before replying in a broad Glasgow accent, 'Aye, there are thairrty-six, an' a bum in evrry one of 'em!' Soon after this encounter, the city gent took her to court for insolence.

✳

On my visit to Glasgow with Mussorgsky's *The Fair of Sorochintsi*, several of the company, including our Second Conductor, Maliniuk (he was Rumanian), stayed in a commercial-type hotel. Before going into the restaurant for lunch one day, he hung his coat on the coat stand, and after the meal found it to be missing. He stormed back into the dining-room and complained bitterly to all of us, stating that if he were not given a replacement coat he would take the next train back to London. It was obvious that he meant what he said, and we knew immediately that the outcome could be disastrous.

We had a quick conference, the result of which was that each of our two character tenors, Herman Simberg and Paul André, offered his own coat pro tem – until Maliniuk could get himself a new one. It seemed that both men had the luxury of two coats each, and so they could afford to be generous. They trotted off to collect them, and on their return Maliniuk very superciliously tried on each coat for size. Simberg's coat, a heavy navy number, was rejected as being too short and not worthy of being worn by a maestro; but Paul's was gorgeous, with a rich, pale blue fleece, large lapels, and a belt. Although Maliniuk looked ridiculous in it, the quality and glamour of the garment obviously won him over, and he accepted it with the air of bestowing a great honour on the donor.

Naturally, Paul was confident that the loan would be for a very short period and that he would have his beloved coat back within a few days. Not so. Maliniuk had no intention of returning it, and he continued to wear it until the end of the tour. Clothes rationing had recently come in with a vengeance, and he evidently saw no reason to waste his coupons on a coat while he had the free use of this beautiful one.

However, the weather was particularly bad that year, and the coat soon lost both its pristine fleecy pile and its pale blue colour. With each day it became drabber, while poor Paul looked more and more depressed. I vividly remember him trailing behind Maliniuk (while wearing a vastly inferior garment) in the vague hope of somehow protecting his beloved coat from the elements. It goes without saying that Maliniuk's aggressive and self-confident manner precluded any possibility of a rapprochement on Paul's side! When, at the end of the tour, the coat was eventually returned to Paul, it bore no resemblance to its former state; and I doubt whether dry cleaning would have brought it anywhere near its original glory.

Soon after our return to London, Simberg and I met for a coffee one Sunday afternoon. While walking down Piccadilly, whom should we see strolling towards us but Maliniuk – dressed in an elegant and superbly cut navy-blue coat. He greeted us in his usual patronizing way, and Simberg and I congratulated him on his new acquisition. 'This isn't a new coat', he replied. 'It's my Sunday best one. I never wear it on any other day.'

✳

My one regret about Glasgow is that during my time there, the name of Charles Rennie Mackintosh (1868–1928) was virtually unknown – as was his wonderful architecture and furniture. Although I often dropped in to the art nouveau tea rooms designed by him, I was unaware of their origins and importance. How much richer and even more personal would Glasgow have seemed to me, had I known of his existence at the time? A few years ago I made a pilgrimage to the city to drink in his art, and wondered yet again how he could have been ignored for so many years.

13

The Fair of Sorochintsi

IN 1941, while entertaining troops in Aldershot, I received a telephone call from a friend, telling me to get back to London as soon as possible to audition for the chorus of Mussorgsky's *The Fair of Sorochintsi*, which was to be staged by the newly-formed Russian Opera Company. The auditions were being held by Anatole Fistoulari at the Wigmore Hall Studios – for many years the hub of musical life in London, having wonderful studios for rehearsals and lessons in addition to the famous recital hall.

My audition was such a success that, instead of joining the chorus, I was nominated by Fistoulari to sing the mezzo lead role of Khivria, alternating with Oda Slobodskaya – then a very celebrated singer in her fifties. He clearly regretted not having heard me earlier, as he had just signed up a rather dubious and inexperienced soprano by the name of Daria Bayan for the *ingénue* role of Parassia. In fact I soon started alternating in that role as well.

The birth of the Russian Opera Company was very interesting and amusing. Three war exiles from Paris, all totally skint and living on their wits, met every now and then for coffee, full of nostalgia and desperation. They were Anatole Fistoulari (conductor), Eugene Iskoldoff (entrepreneur), and George Kirsta (designer). One day one of them had a brainwave: the USSR had recently reneged on Germany to join Britain in the war against Hitler, and everything Russian must therefore be of great interest; so why not put on a Russian opera? They came up with *The Fair of Sorochintsi*, and all that was now needed was the cash and the cast!

A mutual friend put them in contact with a Russo-Jewish gentleman from the East End of London, by the name of Jay Pomeroy (formerly Pomerantz), who had found a quick way of making money on the black market. They met him, told him that they were selling shares costing one hundred pounds each, and asked if he would like to buy one. Although he had probably never even heard the word 'opera', let alone understood the meaning of it, he was game and paid up his one hundred pounds. The three exiles were delighted with their progress and set about spending the money to the best of their abilities!

After a time, having heard nothing further about the undertaking, Pomeroy enquired as to how the project was faring, only to be told that it had stopped dead because no further shareholders had come forward. A business meeting was called, and Pomeroy asked how much capital was needed for the project to take off. When told, he delightedly agreed to finance the whole affair, and in fact seemed rather aggrieved that it had taken them so long to get to the point. Taking a few diamonds from his trouser pocket, he inferred that these could pay for the new company – and so the Russian Opera Company was born!

The cast, collected rather haphazardly, nevertheless consisted of famous and soon-to-be-famous names, including Parry Jones, Otakar Kraus, Edward Boleslawski, Marian Nowakowski and Herman Simberg. As already mentioned, the two principal female roles were sung by Oda Slobodskaya and Daria Bayan, alternating with me and Nina Lenova. The venue was the Savoy Theatre, and the production was designed by Kirsta. The rehearsals, directed by Catherine Devillier (the great ballerina and choreographer, who had taken part in the first production of *The Three-Cornered Hat*), were only for the first cast, so I sat in the stalls and watched.

Kirsta had designed a sensational costume for Slobodskaya: a black beribboned skirt, a sleeveless black velvet jerkin over a bright turquoise blouse with enormous balloon sleeves, caught in the middle with embroidered bands, and a turquoise scarf made into a Ukrainian turban. Slobodskaya took one look at it and said, 'Zat ees not forr mee!' It was therefore thrown in my direction, and with my blonde hair and blue-green eyes, it looked perfect. In fact it received its own special applause at my début. 'Slobs', as she was always known, had another, more prosaic, costume designed for her that was better suited to her rather austere looks. However, when she saw me in her 'cast-offs' she nearly had apoplexy and demanded them back. By then, though, what was mine was mine!

The vocal warming-up of Slobodskaya and Simberg were positively awe-inspiring. Oda would bark like a seal in distress – which, I must admit, can project the voice neatly into the mask if done correctly – and Simberg would saunter up and down the corridors singing his scales to the words *Alles ist geschissen* – his personal mantra – in various tonalities. One never quite knew at what or whom this comment was aimed – if aimed at all!

Very soon I had learnt the part of Parassia, and was sometimes singing it in the matinée in addition to Khivria in the evening performance. I do not remember receiving a word of thanks from anyone for this, nor was there mention of any financial bonus. I was simply a commodity – there to be used. But I was singing at last and fulfilling myself on stage, and for me, that seemed to be enough.

During our run at the Savoy Theatre, Pomeroy – to my amazement – invited me out to lunch and then to the 'Dogs' (the greyhound stadium) at White City. A couple of his business friends joined us, and I suddenly realized that I was being used as a decoy, or simply going to the highest bidder for 'services to be rendered' – or so Pomeroy hoped. He could not have chosen a worse candidate! This was a world completely outside my understanding or acceptance, and I must have been a very damp squib for all concerned. At the end of the afternoon, when whatever was planned had sadly failed, I returned to the theatre with Pomeroy for the evening performance. As he shook hands with me he pushed a crumpled five-pound note into my hand, which I deftly pushed back into his, saying, 'Mr Pomeroy, I do not take tips, but if you wish to increase my salary, I shall not refuse.'

The Savoy had been booked for only three weeks, for who, during wartime, would have imagined a fairly unknown Russian opera, sung in Russian, being an enormous success? It was, however, and the press extolled our production to high heaven. Unfortunately they omitted to mention the brevity of our season, so when we went on tour at the end of the three weeks, a queue was still forming outside the Savoy that went all the way down the Strand to Trafalgar Square.

Our tour was a long one with many problems, mainly because of the double cast and also, subjectively, because I was more and more often singing both leading roles. Right from the start, Jay Pomeroy had taken a distinct shine to Daria Bayan, and she took every possible advantage of her elevated position in the company. Quite apart from very tactlessly arriving in a new outfit every day at a time when clothes were scarce and clothing coupons even scarcer, she often abused her position beyond imagination by demanding to sing every Monday in the provinces so as to be sure of getting press notices in every town.

She also developed a most convenient physical disability, in that her 'monthly curse' would suddenly arrive before the Wednesday or Saturday matinée – two or three times a month! Failing that, she developed food poisoning whenever necessary. It certainly never occurred to *me* not to sing if I ever felt below par, and if it had ever happened, she would certainly never have helped me out.

I was therefore like a yo-yo, always on the alert and ready to step in whenever needed.

After the tour, we returned to London and opened another season of *Sorochintsi* at the Adelphi. By this time both Slobodskaya and Iskoldoff had had enough of Daria's behaviour – she was by now virtually running the company for her own benefit – and had left. A substitute for 'Slobs' was found in Janet Howe, a well-known mezzo and protégé of the late Sir Henry Wood. She arrived as the 'star', treating me and the other members of the cast as dirt. Sharing a dressing-room with me before her first performance, she stripped the room of all of my belongings and put up her frills and furbelows without a 'by-your-leave'.

However, one event ruined her status in possessing the room. I had sung the matinée performance that day, Bayan having *demanded* the evening performance because she smelt the presence of the press at Howe's début; and I had bought some fish for my cat, placed it somewhere in the room, and forgotten to take it home with me. In fact, it had fallen behind the radiator, which was turned full on. Howe did not find the package, and was aware only of the appalling smell getting progressively worse.

The next performance of Khivria on the following day was mine, and when I arrived to make up, Howe was stripping the room bare of all her hangings and belongings. Furious, she complained about the ghastly stench in the room, to which I was able to reply that when I had left it, there had been no smell, and that therefore it must have come with her! From then on, we used separate dressing-rooms.

On another occasion at the Adelphi, I had the afternoon off and, while in the West End, popped into the theatre to buy tickets for my evening performance for some friends. It was around three p.m., and although the curtain had gone up at two-thirty, the first half-hour of the performance consisted of the balletic overture 'The Great Gate of Kiev' from Mussorgsky's *Pictures at an Exhibition*, choreographed by Catherine Devillier. As I entered the foyer I saw, to my horror, a large blackboard on which had been written in chalk, DUE TO THE INDISPOSITION OF DARIA BAYAN, THE ROLE OF PARASSIA WILL BE SUNG BY KYRA VAYNE.

The ballet had ended and there was now a hiatus in the theatre. An announcement had been made, apologizing for a slight delay in beginning the opera. Meanwhile, I had been spotted by the staff of the box office and word had been sent backstage. Within seconds I was almost lifted off my feet by Oscar Pomeroy (Jay's despotic son, now acting as stage manager!) and rushed to my dressing-room. Clothes were thrown on me, and without a vestige of make-up I was 'on'. Obviously, if I had not been passing the theatre at that given moment, the performance would have been cancelled.

At the end of the show I rushed to our cast date list, given out each week and signed by Fistoulari, only to find it missing. No one knew anything about it, and Fistoulari denied all knowledge of it. He screamed at me for not being in constant touch with the theatre, forgetting that I was not an understudy but a member of the *alternate cast* and a lead in my own right.

After the season at the Adelphi, the company was reshuffled. All Pomeroy's contingent left, including La Bayan, but Iskoldoff returned to take a final tour of England. I was now the only official Khivria, but on one occasion the soprano singing Parassia sprained her ankle at the last moment and I had to take on both roles. Fortunately the two characters do not meet on stage, except at the final curtain, and the audience seemed to be unaware that they were getting only one singer for the price of two!

✳

At the end of two London seasons and two long tours of *The Fair of Sorotchintsi* we were definitely past our sell-by date, and by now were on the Number Two Circuit. We had gone through a vast number of conductors and had just acquired a new one, by the name of Berthold Goldschmidt. He was then quite unknown and seemed, in an odd way, completely apart from the company.

He was short in stature with enormous, dark brown, lugubrious, sad, seal-like eyes. I never heard him exchange a single word with any of us, and I have always vividly remembered his air of rather bored resignation and condescension, touched with a considerable degree of sardonic disdain and accusation directed at those on stage. I can also clearly remember his right hand wildly waving his baton while he was immersed in the evening paper lying on his podium, below the audience's eye level.

I found his sense of detachment rather endearing and, secretly, I sympathized with him in his apparent boredom. However, he had a rather gorgeous, blonde, Junoesque wife, so life must have had some compensations for him!

After the tour he seemed to disappear into thin air until, fairly recently, his name hit the news. At the age of ninety, his compositions were at last fully recognized and played in England and Germany to enormous acclaim. He became a great hero and so, right at the end of a long life, tasted the success he so truly deserved. It suddenly all makes sense now, but how sad that his success came so late. For some, however, it does.

*

When *Sorochintsi* was finally over, Pomeroy gave birth to the Cambridge Opera Company in order to further the career of Madame Bayan. A first on his list of productions was Rimsky-Korsakov's *Tsar Sultan*. Pomeroy called me in to discuss contracts and stipulated that he would engage me on one condition: that, at a special press conference, I would inform the journalists that he had paid for all my vocal training and that all I had achieved I owed to him. My struggle to pay for my voice being trained, and my survival in this cesspool, had cost me too much to give the benefit to someone like Pomeroy, so I never had the honour of being in the cast of the Cambridge Opera Company, which had, apart from Daria Bayan, some pretty big artists: Mariano Stabile, the two Murray brothers, Ian Wallace, Margherita Grandi, and Marian Nowakowski.

Walter Susskind

During the run of *The Fair of Sorochintsi* we were in need of a co-*répétiteur*, Slavonic if possible. We had heard mention of the young Walter Susskind, but most of what had been spoken about him was gossip. The latest story was that he was not only an addicted lady's man but also quite adept with a whip; and on one recent occasion he had indulged this little vice over-enthusiastically. The screams – for real – of the lady in question had prompted the neighbours to call the police, who arrived in full force and found Walter 'in action'. He received a strong reprimand, and his work permit was revoked indefinitely.

Walter was a great friend of the baritone Otakar Kraus – they had escaped from Czechoslovakia at the same time – and the latter was very distressed by the outcome of the whip incident. He confided this to several people and it eventually came to the notice of Eugene Iskoldoff, who went to a great deal of trouble to speak on Walter's behalf and to vouch for his value as a musician. Succeeding, he engaged him as our *répétiteur*. Walter, of course, later became a very distinguished conductor.

Personally, I was delighted by his involvement in *Sorochintsi*. His musicianship was superb, and he helped me enormously. I also found him enchanting and extremely attractive, with a great warmth and sense of humour. The fact that he was satyric, and virtually the male equivalent of a nymphomaniac, did not bother me in the least, for we had a perfectly platonic relationship. For example, if we found digs that included cooking facilities, he and I would often share our meals together – I cooking and he eating enthusiastically. What he did in his private life was no concern of mine.

Then one day, while having tea together in my lovely digs in Glasgow, he suddenly blurted out, 'Aren't you perturbed that I've never made a pass at you?' I replied that the question had vaguely crossed my mind but that I had not given the matter much thought. He then explained that he had never made a pass at me, and never would, because he had never been refused by any woman. He knew that I would be the first one to do so, and he could not cope with such rejection. So that was that, and back we went to our lovely platonic relationship.

Little did he know how wrong he was! I might easily have succumbed, for I found him devastatingly attractive and would have been hard-put to brush him aside. However, luck was on my side, and I did not have to face such a decision. But, needless to say, he went through the rest of the ladies in the company like diarrhoea.

After *Sorochintsi* closed, Walter and Otakar Kraus joined the Carl Rosa Opera Company. One evening I attended a performance that he was conducting, and afterwards went backstage to congratulate him. As soon as he saw me, and before even greeting me, he announced very peremptorily that in no way must I ask him for help, his policy being never to help anyone. In fact nothing could have been further from my mind, and I felt most embarrassed.

Walter made a big career in Australia, America, Canada and of course England. He was among the 'Greats', and always had a very young lady in tow – either his latest wife or a passing fancy. While I was in the States I wrote to congratulate him on his latest professional success in New York, but received no reply. Moving on to Canada, I auditioned with great success for the CBC, only to be asked if I knew Walter Susskind, who was their conductor. I hesitated before saying yes, and was then told that without his approval, one had no chance whatsoever. Remembering his backstage warning, I withdrew.

Strange how sometimes a friendship can be almost harmful; and it is not always *who* one knows, but *how* one knows them … However illogical Walter's grudge against me, it was a telling one. And I wonder whether a favour from me would in fact have been reciprocated. Somehow, I doubt it.

15

Eugene Iskoldoff

I HAD BEEN AWARE, ever since the start of *Sorotchintsi,* that Eugene Iskoldoff was very attracted to me. But although I was rather flattered, I ignored his advances. We seemed worlds apart, and he was more than twenty years my senior. I was very much against compromises in my life, and to have accepted him would have been an *enormous* compromise that I was not prepared to make. During our final tour of *Sorotchintsi* there were fewer singers in the cast, and Iskoldoff and I were thrown together more than before.

On my return from this final tour in 1943, I began to find the situation at home untenable. My father and sister showed not the slightest interest in what was obviously a very difficult career path for me to follow. (Every time I returned from touring, I would be handed a bill for a third of all expenses incurred in running the family flat, despite the fact that I lived away most of the time and had my own very heavy personal expenses on tour.) Father also started to look at other singers and to ask me why, when 'so and so' was making it, I was not? The reasons were often obvious, but he would seldom recognize them; and when he did, he seemed to ignore them.

One day he seriously insulted me and I knew I could take no more. I packed what I could and left home, never to return. There was no one I could turn to but Iskoldoff. Needless to say, he was delighted, and so our life together began – both privately and publicly. This was my first conscious, serious compromise, and one that I did not make lightly. True to my belief, I never made another.

It was wonderful to be with someone who seemed to care for me and who could also give me the career that I felt was my due. Alas, our physical relations died even before they were born; for in this area we were completely incompatible. But we continued to live under the same roof, finding in each other complementary companionship. I am sure that he was unfaithful to me, but what my eye did not see, my heart did not know. And that seemed to be the solution. I later learned, however, that what *I* did not see was nevertheless visible to outsiders.

Iskoldoff had great talents as an entrepreneur, but once a contract was signed, he lost all interest in it and simply moved on to the next thing. This was the bitter price I paid – without understanding, at the time, its full portent. Whenever I went to fulfil the contract that had been signed on my behalf, I went alone. There was nobody to cushion me from any problems that might arise, nobody to see that I was given my proper position and had the correct publicity and costumes. And nobody even to keep me company!

Worse still, Gene was never there to follow up the success I achieved (I myself was hopeless at business transactions). I was more vulnerable than any singer in my position should have been, and I suffered deeply. Wherever I went, I seemed to be the perpetual outsider, and I simply assumed that this was how it was supposed to be.

16

Gay Rosalinda

I N 1945 Bernard Delfont staged a glamorous production of *Gay Rosalinda*, an English version of Strauss's *Die Fledermaus*, at the Palace Theatre. The conductor was Richard Tauber, and Ruth Naylor the protagonist, with Cyril Richards as Eisenstein and Peter Graves as Orlovsky. The soubrette role of Adèle was sung by a Viennese escapee from Hitler, Irene Ambrus. She was already in her late forties, with a slightly edgy singing voice but a most ebullient personality. She was the pivot of the whole production, having a rich boyfriend who had financed it. Furthermore, a close coterie of fellow refugees surrounded her – they included Tauber, Leontine Sagan (the Viennese director, famous for her film direction), Elena Gerhardt (the great singer and now a vocal coach), and Alfred Kalmus (the music publisher).

The show opened with a huge fanfare but soon started showing cracks. Ruth Naylor, a well-known opera singer from Sadlers Wells, red-haired and charismatic, did not have a very firm technique, and it soon started to let her down. Her voice simply could not cope with the strain of nightly performances (plus two matinées), and very soon the gorgeous csárdás was out! Auditions for a replacement were held urgently, and I sang for Tauber and Delfont. Both showed their delight and engaged me on the spot.

The next day, I was called to the office to sign the contract with Bernard Delfont and to commence two weeks of rehearsals forthwith. The first thing I noticed about the contract was that, instead of the usual 'two weeks' notice' clause, it read 'for the run of the play'. I realized at once that a long London run and a lengthy subsequent tour could seriously hamper my burgeoning career, and I told Delfont that I would prefer to have the 'two weeks' notice' clause instead. He looked angry, and answered sharply, 'Take it or leave it.' I suggested calling in Iskoldoff to negotiate for me, but Delfont would not agree to this, explaining that he never dealt with agents.

The opportunity of taking over a leading role at one of the most prestigious theatres in the West End was too great for me to pass up, so I signed the contract and waited for Delfont to do the same with his counterpart. Instead, he informed me that *his* contract would be sent to me in a few days' time. I immediately realized the irregularity and illegality of this whole procedure, and was aware that danger lay ahead.

The following Monday, when I arrived at the Palace Theatre to commence rehearsals, I was astonished to find that the stage was empty except for one young man – Ivor Hughes, the stage manager. He informed me that he would take me through the part and read the cues, male and female, from the script. I was staggered that there would be no rehearsals with fellow artists. Instead, for the following two weeks, I was to learn the moves by watching every performance from the front of the house. I persevered in this bizarre set-up, and became good friends with Ivor.

Two or three days after signing my contract, I received Delfont's. It had a *nota bene* in the left hand margin that read, 'The Management has the right to give this artist two weeks' notice.' I was stunned. It was beyond my comprehension that anything so illegal could be forced upon an artist. I could not accept such corrupt practices, and my instinct told me that I had to take the contract straight to Equity. Alas, I demurred. Could I take all that would be involved? Could I endure the legal proceedings, the adverse publicity, and the lethal power wielded by Delfont? Where would it lead? Once again, I resigned myself to the situation. However, it was a dilemma that I have often thought about since. I deeply regretted that I did not take up the cudgels, but could I have won against such odds? Worse shocks were in store!

Our unconventional rehearsals continued until the day of my début. As yet, I had not met a single one of my colleagues. Neither had I had even a piano rehearsal with Tauber. I had been unable to get the feel of my costumes, most of which had trains that swished around my feet, and I went on stage 'cold'. I still do not know how I achieved what I did: my performance went off without a hitch, and I sang my role as if born to the part. For two blissful weeks I *was* Rosalinda; the reviews were brilliant, and I thought I was made.

At the end of those two weeks, as I arrived at the theatre for a Saturday matinée, I found a letter waiting for me. It stated, 'The Management hereby gives Miss Kyra Vayne two weeks' notice, as from today's date.' Riveted to the spot, I stared unbelievingly in front of me. A colleague, James Ethrington, was passing by and saw my condition. He asked me what the matter was, and I simply handed him the letter to read. With a look of infinite pity on his face, he put his arms around me and said, 'But darling, didn't you know?' When I asked him what he meant, he told me the unbelievable truth.

For the past three weeks the entire cast, under the direction of Leontine Sagan, had been rehearsing at the Cambridge Theatre, which had been specially rented for this purpose. These rehearsals were taking place for the benefit of Tara Barry, a pupil of Elena Gerhardt, who, without any stage experience whatsoever, was going to take over the role of Rosalinda at the end of my short contract. It seems impossible that neither Ivor Hughes nor I had got wind of this, but even though he was in the theatre every day and stayed in close contact with all the members of the staff and the cast, he did not know a thing about it. This was the reason for the late and illegal contract from Delfont! It had been held back until he was sure that Miss Barry was capable of carrying out the role.

On discovering the situation, I immediately went to see Tauber in his dressing-room. I knocked, entered, and said, 'Mr Tauber, I have just received a letter terminating my contract as from a fortnight's time. Are you in agreement with this?' He went chalk-white, covered his face with his hands, and muttered, 'Ziss is nossing to do wiz me, nossing. Pliss leave me, pliss leave me.' I realized that he, too, was only a tool in the hands of those wielding the power, and that there was no help to be had from him.

Somehow, I managed my two performances that day, and then went home, ready to die. As soon as possible I made an appointment to see Bernard Delfont, in the hope of finding the answer to this unbelievable enigma. To my question, 'Why have I been given notice?', he replied, 'A beautiful voice is not enough. What you also need is cash.' At this point he rubbed his thumb against his fingers to make the 'money' sign, and added, 'Tara Barry has paid a very large sum of money for the privilege of singing Rosalinda.'

The remaining two weeks of my contract passed in a blur, and when I left at the end I did so in the knowledge that I had allowed Delfont a shattering victory that I had in no way contested. I had tried to the best of my ability to forget the horror of what had happened, always hoping to be given a proper chance to fulfil myself to the best of my potential. Miss Tara Barry was a pedestrian Rosalinda – gauche, with little elegance and no panache. But of course, she was a far more acceptable foil for Irene Ambrus's limited talents than I could ever have been! The show closed sooner than it might have done, after a tour of the provinces. Tara Barry never appeared in any other show or theatrical enterprise. Her stardom was short-lived but, one hopes, worth her financial outlay!

*

The sequel to the story of *Gay Rosalinda* came in 1994 when a freelance television producer became interested in making a documentary about my life. After listening to my tale of the *Rosalinda* saga, he decided to visit the Palace Theatre and to get what information he could, with a view to an interview and a video filmed *in situ*. It was there that he met Graham Cruikshank, an archivist who, some years earlier, had been engaged to research the long and interesting history of the Palace by its new owner, Andrew Lloyd Webber. The theatre had in fact been built by Gilbert and Sullivan as a venue for English opera – which role it never fulfilled, instead housing ballet, Variety and musical shows.

Graham had been able to trace nothing about *Gay Rosalinda* except for a photograph of Richard Tauber and the orchestra, taken from the circle, and a few programmes bearing my name. But by a coincidence, he had heard that a collection of theatrical memorabilia, including something from *Rosalinda*, was to be auctioned. He attended the auction and came away with two costume designs by P. & J. Simmonds Ltd. In the right hand corner of the design he read:

'GAY ROSALINDA'
MISS KYRA VAYNE.

Who was Kyra Vayne? At that time, no one knew. Graham published a short history of the theatre, illustrated with photographs of artists who had participated in its many and varied productions, and the two costume designs bearing my name appeared on the last page, together with photos of Pavlova and Nijinsky. He also mounted an exhibition in the foyer of the theatre, and the two costume designs were the only memoirs of *Rosalinda*.

When Graham met the TV producer and heard him mention my name, he nearly passed out with excitement. He rushed into the next room and returned clutching, in his shaking hands, the two costume designs. Later, when he actually met me, he was almost in tears. For him, I was like a ghost materializing before his eyes.

After all the skulduggery and enormous sums of money that passed hands, I am the only remaining proof that *Gay Rosalinda* ever took place. What happened to all the material that contributed to this production, and to all the photographs of it that must have existed? Again, I wonder what the outcome might have been, had I fought for my rights so many years ago.

17

Conflict in Cardiff

ONE OF THE HAPPIEST days of my professional life came in 1946 when I auditioned in the famous Crush Bar at Covent Garden for both the Dublin Opera Company and the newly-formed Welsh National Opera. I was a great success, and came away with contracts to sing in *La Forza del Destino* in Dublin and in *La Traviata* and *Il Trovatore* for the inaugural season of the Welsh National.

I had originally learned *Traviata* in Italian, and now had to relearn it in English. However, at the very last moment I was given a completely different translation that the Welsh National wanted to use for their production, and so I had to learn the opera for a third time – in very great haste. Even bigger problems were in store.

Although I was fully aware that the company had been formed only recently, I did not realize that the producer, the chorus, the smaller parts and the second conductor, Haydn Jones, were all amateurs. The only professionals were the principal singers – including Victoria Elliott, Walter Midgley, Roderick Jones, Anthony Marlowe, Arnold Davies and myself – and the first conductor, Edward Renton. Furthermore, the administrative staff was made up entirely of business people who were concerned with commercial and nationalist, rather than artistic, considerations.

After a few days Renton called me for a piano run-through of *both* my roles – *La Traviata* in the morning and, following a one-hour lunch break, *Il Trovatore* in the afternoon. I could not believe my ears, and explained as tactfully as possible that it was, regrettably, an impossible task to rehearse two roles that are so demanding and diverse – both dramatically and vocally – with only an hour's break between them. In fact, I pointed out, it would be highly dangerous for me to attempt this, given that it would exhaust my voice and that the opening night was looming. Renton disagreed and was furious, but refused to discuss the matter further with me.

A compromise could easily have been reached by moving the afternoon rehearsal to the evening, thus giving me a respite of five to six hours. But instead, and unbeknown to me, Renton went to the management and 'protested' me: he took *Traviata* away from me on the grounds of my refusal to carry out his orders, thereby convincing the administration of my 'incompetence' and 'unprofessionalism'.

Because the Welsh National was an amateur company, there was not a soul within it who understood my predicament and to whom I could have gone for advice or help. Renton was also artistic director of the company, and so his word was law. He was married to Sir Alan Lascelles's daughter and was obviously extremely well connected. But although still quite young, he looked unkempt, drank heavily, and chain-smoked. In fact he had about him a sense of tremendous insecurity, and attempted to camouflage his defensiveness with exaggerated arrogance.

So, from an exalted position in the company, with two wonderful roles to my name, I was, in a flash, relegated to a position of disgrace without any chance of redemption – something extremely painful for me to accept. As far as my precious *Traviata* was concerned, I was forced to throw in the towel, and the role went to Victoria Elliott, who was singing Rosalinda in the company's production of *Die Fledermaus*.

I very soon realized that I had unwittingly and unwillingly played into Renton's hands. Panic-stricken by the prospect of directing his first ever *Traviata*, he needed to boost his flagging confidence, and was therefore determined to conduct the opera with an 'old-hander' rather than with someone making her début in the production. Elliott was, after all, a pillar of Sadlers Wells Opera, and had sung Violetta many times.

I nevertheless watched the performances of *Traviata* with great interest, and was both bemused and incredulous at the moment in Act Four when Violetta painfully gets out of bed to greet Armand for the last time: Victoria Elliott climbed out of bed wearing four-inch silver evening sandals! Furthermore, in *Die Fledermaus* she did not use the customary mask as a disguise, but instead wore Edna Everage sunglasses, liberally embellished with plastic flowers, that curved upwards into her hairline. How could I possibly have competed with such consummate artistry?

I sang *Trovatore* with Anthony Marlowe as Manrico and Arnold Davies as the Conte di Luna. The conductor, Haydn Jones, was a delightful man – obviously rather 'green', overanxious, and touchingly keen. He loved my voice and responded to me with enormous enthusiasm, so much so that one evening, at the start of the Miserere scene, he froze in a trance. His conducting arm was raised, motionless, in the air, the pages of his score were left un-turned, and his gaze was riveted on me. I could sense the orchestra slowing up and losing rhythm, so I walked to the very edge of the stage, raised my voice, and stamped a kind of fandango. Suddenly Haydn came to life again and quickly turned the pages, and we were back in business.

18

Scandinavia and the USA

N ICOLAI KOUDRIAVTZOFF, a great friend and ex-colleague of Eugene Iskoldoff, came over to England from Canada in 1947. He was a partner in a seemingly flourishing enterprise called American Canadian Artists Incorporated, whose American division was run by Michel Kachouk, also a friend of Gene and a well-known entrepreneur before the war, mostly in connection with Chaliapin.

Koudriavtzoff heard me sing and was extremely enthusiastic. He saw in me a star in the making and remarked that, following the recent tragic death of Grace Moore, he saw her mantle fitting me superbly. He signed me for two concerts in Toronto and Montreal the following year, with the Rochester Philharmonic conducted by Erich Leinsdorf. Prior to that would be a Carnegie Hall recital, and on the success of this would depend a subsequent tour of the States. There was no way in which recitalists could be given a tour, or in fact any other engagements in America, without their initiation at Carnegie Hall, and the one condition of our deal was that half of the fee for renting the hall would be our responsibility. It was that or nothing.

It was now urgent for Gene and me to raise sufficient cash to make this dream a reality. He went off to Scandinavia to renew old contacts and returned with a superb contract for me: singing Variety at the famous China Theatre in Stockholm, as well as in Gothenburg and Oslo and at the Tivoli Gardens in Copenhagen. This was a very big deal, and the money excellent. Apart from having visited Ireland, this was going to be my first trip outside Britain, and I was in seventh heaven – so much so that I kept dreaming of Stockholm in magical colour. On arrival, I experienced an amazing sense of *déjà vu* that was indeed like walking from a dream into reality. The brightness of the light, the blue of the sea, and the amazing colours of the tiled rooftops, were not only blinding in their beauty but seemingly familiar.

At the China Theatre I was starring with Stéphane Grappelli and Django Rheinhardt (Maurice Chevalier had been there the previous month), and I remember how awestruck I was to see enormous posters featuring my photograph plastered on every wall of the many public loos in the town – like small iron pergolas painted a bright green. This, surely, was real fame!

While in Stockholm we received, out of the blue, an unexpected visit from Michel Kachouk. At first sight of him I cringed. He was short and obese, with a heavily jowled face, an oily manner, and great conceit. He was also a womanizer, promising the earth to any young, aspiring artist in any field – I once saw him pounce on a very attractive young ballet dancer who was obviously seduced by his reputation and hypnotized by his dulcet tones. It was immediately obvious that Kachouk and I did not hit it off. He expected from me the same adulation that he was used to receiving, and openly resented both my rejection of his 'charms' *and* Gene's prerogative over me and my talent. He never bothered to hear me sing or watch me perform, and very soon started to undermine my confidence, whenever and however he could.

The reason for his sudden appearance soon became obvious: he smelt cash, and simply had to make some of it his own, by hook or by crook. Unbeknown to me, he bargained with Gene to obtain our half of the Carnegie Hall rental in advance, with promises on his mother's life that we would get it back intact on our arrival in New York. Gene, fool that he was, fell for this, and Kachouk soon left, far richer than when he had arrived.

Before travelling from Sweden to Denmark I was asked by Dietrichson, a very prestigious and reputable concert agent, to take a small package to some friends of his. He explained that he would be extremely grateful if I would help him in this way, and because I wanted to consolidate our excellent relationship, I agreed immediately. Arriving at Copenhagen, I was met by his friends and only then discovered that the package contained some very valuable diamonds. I was shattered to realize that I had innocently joined the smuggling trade and put myself in great danger; and a perfunctory 'thank you' was all the reward I received for my errand.

✳

After my stint in Scandinavia we returned to London to cool our heels before sailing for New York – a date had now been fixed for my Carnegie Hall recital. We had booked a passage on the *Queen Mary*, and arrived at Portsmouth to find a major strike in progress. There was a delay of around three to four days, and when we finally sailed, the weather was appalling. Most of the passengers succumbed to the elements, and when, so soon after the austerity of wartime, they were faced with twice-daily menus of a richness defying belief, they gave up and retired to their cabins for the rest of the journey. Gene and I were more abstemious and therefore remained on our feet! We also made a casual acquaintance with a very pleasant couple on the ship; I mention them here because they were to play a major role in later events.

About a mile from New York harbour I was appalled to see package after package of food, including whole lengths of smoked salmon and large joints of meat, being thrown into the sea; health regulations demanded this, but so soon after the deprivations of wartime it seemed an almost sacrilegious act.

Arriving in the city itself, the first shock for me was a peremptory message at our hotel from Erich Leinsdorf, requesting my presence at his Forest Hills home the following day. I realized at once that he wished to hear me sing before committing himself to my appearance under his baton. For more than ten days I had not been able to practice vocally, and I was therefore taking an enormous risk. However, it was useless to protest, so off I went with a hope and a prayer. I was to sing 'Ernani, involami' from *Ernani*, 'Depuis le jour' from *Louise*, and Tatyana's Letter Scene from *Eugene Onegin* – quite a marathon – but fortunately my voice did not let me down, and Leinsdorf seemed delighted.

Kachouk soon turned up with appalling news: there would be no Carnegie Hall recital. He had spent our half of the rental fee *and* the other half that he and Koudriavtzoff were liable for. More dreams shattered ... and more agonizing heartbreak for me. With the usual Sod's Law, Koudriavtzoff had very recently brought over to Canada a large ballet company from Europe – the first after the war. Alas, business was bad, and he lost what capital he had. He was broken. And here I must point out that he was an exception to the rule; he was a decent, honest, enterprising man, a real gentleman, who had been powerless to prevent this disaster but who still felt tremendously guilty towards me.

Gene now went off in a wild attempt to sell both me and the erstwhile famous pianist Malczujinsky. But his luck was out, and our situation was becoming extremely fragile. Kachouk was still jibing at me, inferring that I was somehow to blame for the situation because I was so untalented. I developed complete insomnia, and for weeks was like a zombie, praying for just a few minutes of real sleep. Yet because of the body's amazing ability to compromise by accepting such drastic changes to daily life, I almost got used to not sleeping. However, any ambitions that I might have had evaporated, and, without friends or money, I simply wished my days away.

Alone in New York, in an impersonal room on the twentieth floor of a fairly humble Manhattan hotel, I would have jumped out of the window had I not been such a coward. All that was preventing me was a narrow ledge. Financial problems are the one thing that can destroy me, and New York is certainly not the place to have them!

Eventually Leinsdorf gave instructions for me to go to Rochester, the home of the orchestra, to run through my arias with his assistant. Once again I was panic-stricken, and once again, by some miracle, my voice answered me. I vividly remember my astonishment on hearing the young accompanist say, 'Your musicianship is superb.' For a moment I felt alive and sane again, but this soon passed.

Three weeks later, still suffering from complete insomnia, I arrived in Toronto for my concert with Leinsdorf and the Rochester Philharmonic. The venue was the Maple Leaf Gardens, which seated seventeen thousand. It took me five minutes to enter or leave the concert platform, but after I had done this several times to thunderous applause, I once again felt the joy of being alive and able to give myself to the public. My Montreal concert was also a great success, and I started to live a more normal life.

While in Toronto I made a number of useful contacts, and was even approached by an agent through whom I signed a contract for an important radio commercial sponsored by Borden's Milk. This was to be recorded in six months' time. It seemed once again that I *could* sell myself when I had the courage. But then it was back to New York, and another major financial crisis soon occurred. I lapsed into my usual waiting for Godot, for there seemed no breakthrough from Gene's side. Desperate consultations now began, and hints were made that I should return to London before a real disaster struck.

In a last act of desperation I somehow managed to pick up the courage I thought I had lost, and contacted the famous musical producer Schubert. He listened to me, was very enthusiastic, and suggested that I wait until the right opportunity arose. I also auditioned for the St Louis Light Opera Company, whose musical director, Edwin MacArthur, had for many years been Kirsten Flagstad's accompanist. He, too, was most enthusiastic about me, and remarked that my voice was the nearest in quality to Flagstad's that he could remember hearing. He signed me for a contract which, again, was to commence in six months' time. For reasons best known to himself, Kachouk came to both these auditions, and

71

afterwards demanded to know why I had not told him how talented I was! The irony was almost beyond imagination.

By this time, our money had completely run out – hardly surprising, since we had been living in hotels for a long period. Gene had just enough to buy me a return passage on, again, the *Queen Mary*, and since I knew there was no way that he and I could exist together in New York until my contracts matured, I had no choice but to agree to go back to London. Fifty years later, I keep asking myself why and how I got myself into such a devastating situation, and I cannot find a logical reason. I was simply trapped.

The shock of a long-cherished dream crashing around me; the annihilating power of a city like New York; the collapse of a man in whom I had put my faith and trust; these, together with the cold fear of being without a cent, had overpowered me. Even if my voice still stood up to so many tests, it was not enough. I should have freed myself from Gene long ago, but hope, loyalty, pity, and even quite a lot of gratitude bound me to him. An important factor was that, subconsciously, I could not accept being a liability or a responsibility to him – that was against everything I stood for.

So I boarded the *Queen Mary* and returned to London, with only ten pounds in my pocket and nowhere to live. I booked into a small bed and breakfast hotel in Kensington and prepared myself for a new life, however unpleasant. Gene was left without money or hope, and unsuccessfully attempted suicide. One day soon afterwards, in the foyer of his small hotel, he came face to face with the couple we had met on the *Queen Mary* when first sailing to New York. They seemed delighted to see him again, and invited him for dinner.

During the meal he poured out his tale of woe and his ambitions for the future. And if one does not believe in miracles, now is the time to change one's mind. For the couple listened to Gene's story, asked what he had been planning when disaster struck, and learned that he had wanted to put on a musical for Kyra Vayne. They asked him how much money he needed, and when he quoted a figure, they backed him with that sum. As I write this, I can hardly believe the story myself, but it is true.

A few days later I received a sum of money to tide me over until my return to New York, with a promise of more cash to follow. By this time, unfortunately, I had opted out of the two contracts I had signed in America. However, Gene decided to go to Hollywood to try his luck in finding a composer and librettist who would write a musical on a subject that he had cherished since first hearing of it in Russia. The musical was to be called *Amarak*, and I was to play the leading role. He did indeed find a composer, Philip Kadman, and a librettist. Each was brilliant in his own field, but the process was costing a lot of money and Gene was doing his best to spend it all.

He sent me a plane ticket to Hollywood, via New York, so that I could join him there. I arrived bemused and bewildered – Gene was all optimism, and it was very contagious. While plans for *Amarak* were being made, he *could* have tried to sell me – in what was a very lucrative market. But once again he put me 'on ice' while we awaited the realization of the musical. I stayed for some days in a top class hotel, and then took a small apartment on Sunset Boulevard. By this time Gene had made quite a few wealthy contacts, and it seemed as if everything was waiting to take off.

Very soon afterwards Gene decided to go to New York for further negotiations, and left me behind. Once again, I was in limbo. The thought of selling myself in Hollywood without him or any other agent was quite beyond me – the town's reputation was very frightening, and I was not prepared to fight the system on my own. Despite this, there always remained a very strong feeling that, to quote Gene's favourite Russian saying, 'Even the broom can shoot'. And I certainly had the potential to be a winner *if* ... However, having wasted at least three months in Hollywood, leading a kind of blissful suburban existence of *dolce far niente* in the world's most celebrated venue for a quick fix of world fame (and millions), I therefore left for New York and Gene.

Life there was also tolerable. Gene was happily living through the money earmarked for the musical, whose music and libretto had now been completed. Both had enormous potential for success – again, *if* ... This time, he had acquired a substantial circle of friends, and so life seemed far more normal and interesting than on my previous visit to the city. I was now able to do a round of theatres and to visit the opera and art galleries; and, without the shattering pall of depression hanging over me, I could appreciate them all. And of course there was also a feeling of optimism that, this time, Gene knew what he was doing and had found the right course towards the golden carrot dangling in front of our noses.

At a party in New York at which I sang I met Kerensky, head of the Duma and the provisional post-Revolution government in Russia until he was deposed by the Bolsheviks. A moderate, his policy had been to wrest autocratic power from the Tsar (*Rex est lex*), rather than having him killed or exiled. I found it awe-inspiring to come face to face with someone so central in that ghastly struggle for power in my native country, and I was even more awestruck when he likened the quality of my singing and interpretation to that of Chaliapin.

After a few weeks Gene decided to return to London and to put into action the fruits of his stay in New York. I found a flat in Seymour Street, near Marble Arch, and picked up what contacts I had left behind. I was soon broadcasting and giving concerts again, and I won a contract for Rimsky-Korsakov's *The Invisible City of Kitezh* at the Liceu, Barcelona. Meanwhile, Gene was doing his damnedest to launch the musical, with a great deal of hope but little to show for it.

19

The Prodigy

W HILE FULFILLING my Variety engagement at the famous
China Theatre in Stockholm, I was staying in the same hotel
(the laid-back Castel) as the newly-discovered conductor, the Italian
child prodigy Pierino Gamba. He was then about eight years old,
and a very quiet, pallid-looking boy.

He was sharing a hotel room with his parents, and I was amused
to hear that they had brought their own provisions, consisting
mostly of pasta, which they cooked on a small paraffin stove in
their room. The staff of the hotel restaurant were most concerned
when they found out about this, and put Pierino's pale complexion
and rather listless manner down to his stodgy diet. Under one pre-
text or another they enticed him down to the kitchen, where the
chef would stuff him with steak and other delicacies, begging him
not to tell his parents.

Pierino was in Stockholm to conduct a very important concert
with the Swedish Radio Orchestra, and I had the privilege of being
invited to the first rehearsal. Sitting in the stalls, I felt completely
overwhelmed by the sight of this orchestra, noticing the look of
angry resentment on the faces of the rather elderly musicians and
sensing the almost oppressive animosity towards the small figure
of Pierino as he climbed up to take his place on the podium. One
could almost cut the atmosphere with a knife; it was full of tension
and hostility.

Then a startling thing happened. The boy, dressed rather like
Little Lord Fauntleroy in a short jacket and short trousers, suddenly
pulled himself up and, before my very eyes, grew into his role of
orchestral maestro. He then briskly tapped his baton against his
music stand and, with a great flourish, started to conduct in the
most incredibly decisive and professional manner. He had no music with him, and the whole programme was a feat of memory.

I glanced at the instrumentalists and was deeply moved by the
sudden change in their attitude. The resentment and anger were
gone, and in their place were looks of utter amazement and admiration. During a pause Pierino spoke to the percussionists and
asked them something; then he climbed down from the rostrum
and made for the timpani. Having obviously found them out of

tune, he carefully tuned them himself, to his own and everyone else's delight. Seeing this was one of the great experiences of my life, and I would not have missed it for anything.

In between rehearsals and performances, Pierino could be found in the hotel lounge, sitting by himself and doing his homework with total concentration. He was quite oblivious to the chatter of voices and the clinking of coffee cups around him. One day some friends came to visit me at the hotel with their very large Alsatian dog. Pierino was walking down the stairs as my friends were going up, and at the sight of the dog he went white. Panic-stricken, he flattened himself against the wall in an attempt to avoid the animal. The great Indian dancer Ram Gopal was performing in Stockholm at this time and also staying in our hotel; he had been at the bottom of the stairs and had seen Pierino's distress. He was very intrigued by this, and I remember him saying to me afterwards, 'Someone should search through the past to see which young musician was killed or injured by a dog. Pierino is obviously his reincarnation, as a prodigy.'

During one of my own performances at the China I was amazed to see Pierino sitting in the front stalls, gazing up at me with wonder in his eyes. I must admit that I felt embarrassed by the material I was performing in front of this young genius. After the performance, his little figure appeared at my dressing-room door, asking in the most humble tone if I would please autograph his programme! I was also amused to hear that after his successful tour of Scandinavia conducting regional orchestras, he returned home to Italy in a long private train crammed full of fabulous gifts bestowed on him by adoring audiences.

I have always cherished my memories of Pierino, and was sad to learn that, as sometimes happens in the case of prodigies, he never made the great career for which he had so much potential. His name has cropped up from time to time but, apart from a few recordings, not in anything important and rarely outside Italy.

20

Kitezh

URING THE 1940s I made a private recording of the two
arias sung by Jaroslavna in Borodin's opera *Prince Igor*. The
tapes were used as audition material for the first post-war
International Opera Season at the Liceu, Barcelona in 1949, and,
thanks to their success, I was signed to sing the part of Fevronia in
Rimsky-Korsakov's *The Legend of The Invisible City of Kitezh*. This
was the first of the Russian operas to open the season, and it was
followed by Italian, French and German companies. The Russian
operas that were going to follow *Kitezh* were *Khovanshchina* and *Le
Coq d'Or*, and it was therefore a contractual must for me to sign, in
addition to Fevronia, for the small part of Emma in *Khovanshchina*
and for the voice of the golden cockerel.

I had never seen *Kitezh* and knew very little about it, so I had to
concentrate very hard on learning the role of Fevronia. I studied it
first with Vilem Tausky, and was then advised by the Paris agent,
Nadia Bouchonnet, to have further coaching from either Georgi
Pozemkowsky, who had been a very great Grishka (the comic tenor
character in *Kitezh*), or from Maria Kouznetzova, a famous
Fevronia who had sung the role at the opera's première in St
Petersburg. Both singers were now retired and living in Paris.

Nadia Bouchonnet arranged an appointment with Pozemkowsky
for me, and on my arrival in Paris I went to the Rachmaninov
Academy to meet him. He was a little late, and made a very theatrical entrance into the studio, his coat slung over his shoulders.
He was tall and elegant, with a great physical presence. He looked
me up and down critically and, without further ado, explained that
he would like to be paid *in advance* for his services. I was appalled
by this, as I knew he had a serious drink problem, and I realized
that once the cash was in his hot, sticky hand, no coaching would
be forthcoming from him. I replied that this arrangement would
not be practicable and that I could therefore not agree. He snorted
like a racehorse and strode out of the studio, slamming the door
behind him and leaving me open-mouthed.

I went straight to Bouchonnet's office, only to find that she had
just received two urgent phone calls. The first was from Maria
Kouznetzova who, having heard through the grapevine of my

arrival in Paris, was anxious to coach me – *free of charge*, if necessary. The second message was from Pozemkowsky, who evidently
had considered the matter further and had rung to say that in lieu
of payment he would be very happy if I ordered, and paid for, two
suits from his Barcelona tailor. The choice of coaches was now
mine, and I naturally chose Kouznetzova (but not for free, of
course). Pozemkowsky was left to gnash his teeth in rage.

Kouznetzova and I had a wonderful working relationship. She
was a tremendous artist with great charisma, and was more than
willing to pass her professionalism on to me. She helped me enormously, teaching me grace and superb deportment. She was also a
delightful, warm woman – and still very beautiful, with a wonderful
skin and elegant figure. Having studied the role of Fevronia with
her, I went on to Barcelona for the rehearsals.

To go off at a slight tangent: Kouznetzova and Pozemkowsky
had been lovers for many years and now, having split up, hated
each other intensely. Kouznetzova's son, Michel Benoit, was artistic
director of the Liceu – thanks to his mother, of course. A few years
earlier she had had her own opera company, and, while on tour in
South America, he gambled away the entire company in one night,
leaving her almost destitute. Notwithstanding this – and, I feel
sure, quite a few more of his pranks – she still doted on him. She
told me that when I met him in Barcelona, the first thing I had to
do was to give him her love, and then to let him know that he need
have no worries about my role because I had studied it in minute
detail with her.

I did exactly as she had asked, but his response horrified me. He
smirked and said, 'Forget whatever my mother taught you. She
hasn't got a clue.' At this point I felt as if something inside me
died; I suddenly despised Benoit, and wept for the life of his
mother – a great singer and artist who had been ruined by too
much love for an unworthy son. She had been married to
Massenet's son and had been one of Puccini's lovers; when she
showed me letters and cards from the latter, I somehow felt as if I
were touching history.

Arriving at the Liceu, I knew nobody and was a complete outsider. We were a 'scratch' company with artists from most of the
Slavonic countries, as well as a few Russian men from Paris who
spent the whole year as taxi drivers, and for whom this season of
opera was the highlight of their calendar, bringing hope and excitement into their lives. My tenor was a Rumanian, and 'Grishka' a
Czech. The latter had no personality at all, no acting ability, and an

uninteresting voice. Furthermore, he did not know his part and had not progressed beyond the first half of the opera. His excuse for this last failing was that the score he had been given had all the pages of the second half missing. The management had no choice but to believe him, to give him another score, and to tell him to learn his part immediately!

Days went by, and still he made no progress at all. And because he was involved in most of my scenes, I was unable to rehearse my part. I could foresee a calamity. As our first night loomed near, he had – unbelievably – got no further, obviously being incapable of learning a part. We were due to open on a Saturday evening, and the night before, the management sent Pozemkowsky a telegram begging him to be at the theatre by the Saturday afternoon to take over the role. He agreed, and it is not difficult to imagine his feelings of triumph! However, he was courteous and helped me as much as he could, and it was wonderful to work with so great an artist.

The opening night was a great success and I had very good 'crits', but something awful was happening to my voice. Although I am loath to describe at length my various attacks of vocal illness, I feel I must recount this one, simply because of its horror and after-effects. Unknown to me, the Liceu in Barcelona was a famous germ-trap and it seemed that every 'gob' ever spat out by the great tenors and baritones down the ages had remained *in situ* and become sanctified on hallowed ground. (Opposite the stage door, across a gloomy corridor, was a door painted with a sign that read VENEREAL DISEASES CLINIC, so the atmosphere was not madly auspicious!) In fact I cannot begin to describe the filth backstage. All those in the know inoculated themselves prior to each operatic season, but alas! I had not been warned, and the moment I put my foot inside the door, that was it.

I began to feel the usual tickling at the back of the throat, then a surfeit of phlegm, and then dryness. Before long I could hardly speak – I had caught laryngitis, tonsillitis, pharyngitis . . . you name it! As rehearsals progressed, my vocal condition deteriorated still further, and by the time *Kitezh* was ready for its première I was ready to die – voiceless! There was nothing I could do, because the Russian operas were opening the International Season and we had no second cast or understudies.

When all the usual remedies failed miserably, the theatre's voice specialist was called in. He took one look at my inflamed and swollen throat, and said that the only thing he could suggest were injections of strychnine, which would force the vocal chords to tighten sufficiently for the sound to come through. As this would be effective for only a short time, it was to be administered immediately before the curtain went up; and I was warned that on no account should I test whether the voice was there before I went on to sing or between acts. If there were no voice there would, of course, be no show. And that would be that.

The role of Fevronia is a very long one, and it opens the opera. Alone on stage, she sings a lengthy and difficult – almost Wagnerian – aria. The test to which I was put was therefore almost beyond imagination. I knew that one of two things would happen that evening: either my voice would make it, or the curtain would immediately come down again, and that would be that. It is hard to imagine my feelings before the curtain went up, except that deep down inside me was the knowledge that, somehow or other, my voice could *not* let me down. And in fact that is how it was. Somehow, my voice answered me. I made it – with the help of strychnine, more of which was pumped into me during each interval. I was a success and my reviews were powerful, and although I was unable to speak between performances, my singing voice never let me down – unbelievable though this may seem.

Unfortunately I had no opportunity for rest, because in addition to *Kitezh* I was singing in *Khovanshchina* and *Le Coq d'Or*. The role of the golden cockerel is usually sung in the wings, but the Liceu's management considered me to be such a glamorous focal point that they felt I should sit with the orchestra. We were under the baton of Anatole Fistoulari, and unfortunately he was anything but a singer's conductor. All that interested him was the overture and orchestral interludes of an opera; time and time again he would rehearse these after whizzing through all the vocal parts.

For the first performance of *Le Coq d'Or* he very foolishly sat me next to the leader of the orchestra, and I did not realize that the first violins played only pizzicato, accompanying the main melody which was played by the woodwind. Therefore, all I could hear from my seat next to the violins was a massive pizzicato crescendo that completely swamped the melody. Without a single cue to my vocal entry, and with no clue whatsoever as to the pitch of my first note, I simply went for what sounded logical, and somehow got away with it. The theme of the golden cockerel is repeated about eight times, each time in a different tonality, so God knows how I managed it. Yet the critics wrote that the best voice in the whole opera was mine!

Notwithstanding my professional success, I was alone in Barcelona at Christmas, and to put into words my own personal misery at that time is impossible. Eating alone in the Grand Hotel was an agony of solitude that I would rather forget, and I found out later that the other guests had placed bets on how long I would remain alone. They had backed the wrong horse!

After I returned home to London my voice was still suffering the after-effects of the strychnine injections, and I began to have more vocal difficulties. The voice itself seemed totally unimpaired, and yet it would suddenly snap without warning on a top note. This kept happening, and I was powerless to prevent it. I became panic-stricken. I consulted the most renowned throat specialists, but they all found nothing physically wrong and told me that the problem was psychosomatic. Although I was not convinced, nothing could be done to help me, and so I had no option but to grin and bear it.

Around this time, Eugene Iskoldoff brought over from Italy three singers with whom I was to form a quartet. I continued to experience enormous vocal difficulty and uncertainty, but somehow managed to hold my own and complete a long tour with this 'Italian Quartet'. For most of the time I was so ill that I had to have complete rest during the day and simply hope that the adrenaline would carry me through each evening's performance – which, thank God, it did.

Several months later I went to Paris to work with Maria Kouznetzova on the role of Tosca, and a friend there took me to see his GP. The doctor examined me, heard my story, and immediately diagnosed my problem as 'dry pleurisy' – an after-effect of my illness and the strychnine injections in Barcelona. He was astonished that I had been able to keep singing for so long, and amazed that my voice had not been permanently destroyed. He suggested acupuncture – almost unheard of in those days, and certainly not available from the average GP – and after one session of treatment from him my voice was back to normal.

21

Parsons and Beecham

I N 1995 a lovely article headed 'The Maestro of NW6' appeared
in a London newspaper. Alongside it was a photo showing
Geoffrey Parsons with a line of great artists standing behind him
and queuing for his services. Vivid memories of this now late,
renowned, accompanist suddenly flooded back.

In the late 1940s the two of us were young and at the beginning
of our careers. As yet, there were only embryonic 'Greats' queuing
up for his services, which then cost five shillings an hour. As well
as being a brilliant accompanist, Geoffrey was ebullient, confident,
dapper and full of humour. We spent many happy hours making
music together.

One day he gave a small party in his flat (in, I think, Maida
Vale), and at the end of the evening someone suggested some music. Geoffrey winked at me and asked, 'Tatyana's Letter Scene?' I
replied, 'Great!', and off we went. We were both in tremendous
form, and just for once we were entertaining for pleasure, not for
cash! Two-thirds of the way through the aria, the doorbell rang.
Geoffrey ignored it and we carried on regardless. The bell rang
again, this time more insistently. Enraged, Geoffrey leapt up to
open the door, only to find two policemen facing him.

One of them said, 'We've 'ad complaints about the noise, and
we've come to stop it.' Geoffrey went white, and his jaw tautened.
'Do you know who we are?', he snapped through gritted teeth.
'Couldn't care less, Guv', replied the bobby. 'Just stop the noise,
OK?' It was just on eleven p.m.

✳

My singing teacher, Mignon Nevada, sang a tremendous amount
with the Thomas Beecham Opera Company before the war, and in
1951 she introduced me to Sir Thomas, who then had a suite in
Grosvenor House. I accepted his invitation to audition for him
there, but found the conditions very difficult to sing in. The sitting-
room was quite small and furnished with very heavy drapes and
thick carpets, which resulted in an acoustic that was unsympa-
thetic, to say the least. However, he seemed pleased with my voice,
and then asked if I would sing some Mozart for him.

By this time I was gasping for something to drink, and so I

tentatively asked Sir Thomas's wife, who was sitting by his side, if it would be possible to have a glass of water. Much to my embarrassment, and therefore to add to my nerves, she rather patronizingly said to him, 'Darling, go and get her a glass of water.' I nevertheless sang my Mozart and Sir Thomas was very pleased, saying that he hoped to be able to work with me in the future.

Later that year the Beecham Opera Company staged Balfe's *The Bohemian Girl* at Covent Garden, and Sir Thomas was strongly in favour of my singing the principal role, Arline. Unfortunately he had already lost his 'clout', and therefore his opinions did not carry sufficient weight; so instead of signing me, the company imported Roberta Peters from the United States. The production was not a huge success; Beecham, as always, was superb, but the cast was considered patchy.

Soon afterwards Sir Thomas was asked to conduct the music for Michael Powell and Emeric Pressburger's film of *The Tales of Hoffmann*. Once again, he was strongly in favour of using me for the principal roles in the opera; but once again his clout was not strong enough. And having contracted another singer, Margherita Grandi, whom they had not yet used, the producers had no choice but to offer her the parts in the film. Sadly, therefore, my promising contacts with Beecham never really bore fruit.

22

Igor and Italy

W HEN I WAS TWENTY-ONE a Russian friend took me to the Concours Hippiques at Olympia, where a troupe of Russian Cossacks from Paris were performing under the name of Les Cosaques Djiguites. Their feats of horsemanship were astounding, and my friend demanded to go backstage to meet them. Painfully shy, I trailed behind her, but the Cossacks were as thrilled to see us as we were to see them. There and then, they named me their mascot and insisted that I came to all their performances around London. Until war broke out, they visited every year, renting a field or open area such as Paddington Green in or around the city, and putting up their tents with a huge marquee in the middle. Inside was an immense meal table, at which I often ate with them.

As much as I had always adored horses, I had never really had any physical or social contact with them, and did not have a clue about riding. When I visited the Cossacks at Sittingbourne, Kent, on one of their tours, it was decided behind my back that the time for my initiation had come. Before I fully realized what was happening, I was lifted onto a gorgeous steed – the gentlest one of all, so I was told. But I had not even had a chance to grab hold of the bridle before the horse, enraged by sensing a philistine on its back, reared and took off like an arrow, travelling at great speed and making straight for some empty sheds at the bottom of the field. The doorway of one of the sheds would have decapitated me had not one of the Cossacks immediately realized the danger; leaping onto a horse, he raced after us and managed to divert my own horse only seconds from disaster. I was numb with panic, and slid onto the ground in a tangled heap. My humiliation was far greater than that of my steed who, with a whinny of disgust, trotted off to pastures new. I had obviously let the side down.

While on tour with *Balalaika* in Liverpool, our paths crossed again. The plot of *Balalaika* is a very sentimental one, and concerns an ex-Cossack officer now working as a doorman in a swish Russian restaurant in Paris. In our production the singer wore the gorgeous white parade Cossack uniform, and I cajoled the management into letting me have half a dozen complementary tickets so that I could invite some genuine Cossacks to the show. They arrived resplendent in their own white parade uniforms, and were given a box that was floodlit in order that the audience could look at the real thing watching their characters on stage.

The racial appearance of the Cossacks was Caucasian and slightly oriental – short in stature and wiry, with trim waists. Their uniform consisted of a tightly-fitting tunic, breeches with a dagger angled through the belt, and high leather boots as soft as gloves. Their agility as riders was indescribable, and they were also superb exponents of the famous Sabre Dance. One Cossack, Stepan, gave a solo performance, dancing on bent toe joints, swirling and leaping with three *very* sharp sabres balanced on his teeth – two lying horizontally with their points meeting in the middle, and the third *upright*, with its sharp point balanced on the other two. In the middle of his wild skirmish he would toss his head, causing one of the daggers to whistle through the air before landing, quivering, on the floor about twelve feet in front of him; this was followed rhythmically by the other two daggers. It was a wondrous sight, and one to be treasured.

On one occasion when I was in Scarborough with the Chauve-Souris revue, our visits to the town coincided once more. Arriving at their venue, I was met by a tall, slim, and extremely handsome young man in Cossack uniform. His name was Igor Semiletoff, and he was the son of a Cossack general (who, like most Russian émigrés in Paris, became a taxi driver) who had enlisted him in the group in order to make a man of him. It was, I am afraid, love at first sight – the first and only time that this has ever happened to me, and probably to Igor as well. We were both dazed, walking around as if in some golden dream, and this became the first romance of my life.

Igor was warned by his colleagues that I was someone special and that he was not to fool around with me. Over the next few months we saw as much of each other as possible, but when war broke out, our dreams fell apart. Being French-born, Igor had no choice but to return to Paris for conscription which, to his shame, he evaded for the duration of the War. He also married his ex-girlfriend and wrote to tell me that it was all over between us. My whole world was bound up in him, and the shock of this announcement was incalculable. I took it very badly, but accepted that somehow my life now had to continue without him. I therefore picked myself up and began to pursue my career.

✳

By 1950 Eugene Iskoldoff and I had been together for about eight years. One day he suggested in a roundabout way that he felt it was time for us to go our separate ways. He was tired of being known as 'Mr Vayne' and felt that I, too, should have my freedom. Although our professional relationship would of course continue, I was now able to start a new personal life. By a strange coincidence, it was at exactly this time that I received a letter from Igor – a rather terrifying one, in fact. The letter had followed me all over London and had finally been delivered to my latest address on my birthday, which seemed almost prophetic.

The contents of the letter gave me a short, sharp indication of the life Igor had been living – hell would be a good description of it. He had behaved pretty appallingly during the eleven years since I had last seen him, abandoning his wife and child early in the marriage. He had also become an alcoholic. But although his life was broken, he wrote that his love for me was unchanged, begging me to give him another chance if I were still unattached. This, he claimed, was his only hope.

The shock of hearing Gene's decision and then of receiving Igor's letter somehow fused together and suggested a new direction for my life. And because my love for Igor had never died, I grabbed at this straw, feeling as if destiny were guiding me. I replied to his letter, telling him that I had decided to give our relationship another chance. However, I had things to do before I could meet him in Paris, for Gene and I were about to travel to Milan to 'suss out' the operatic scene there. He had already floated the idea of an Italian opera company of which I would be an important member.

Italy was enormously exciting and full of great possibilities, but by the time we had arrived there, my mind, stupidly, was on other things. Thoughts of my meeting with Igor and our new life together ousted all my other feelings, and during my three weeks in Milan I did not bother to make any significant new professional contacts. I was simply not interested.

Our hotel was the Marina Scala, opposite the opera house's stage door, and it had a huge courtyard onto which faced all the bathrooms. Vittorio de Sabata was also staying at the hotel and, having caught sight of me, showed an ever-increasing interest by tipping the porters in an attempt to arrange a meeting with me. I was in no mood for an entanglement with the maestro, although I was well aware of the greatness of his name.

Then one day, when I was literally sitting on the loo and trying out my voice, I soared without thinking into a rather spectacular cadenza that finished on a top D. Shortly afterwards the phone in my room rang, and I heard a voice say, 'Maestro de Sabata speaking. Do you realize what you have just sung?' When I replied, 'No, not really', he told me that we simply *had* to meet – I had a magnificent voice, and he had to hear it properly. Caught off my guard, I told de Sabata that Thursday evening would suit me. He replied that he had an *Aida* dress rehearsal that evening. Because I was already opposed to the whole idea of auditioning for him, I remained resolute and explained that there would be no other opportunity to meet him, for I was leaving Italy on the Thursday night.

To my amazement, he was prepared to postpone the dress rehearsal, and we arranged a time to meet. He was waiting for me at the stage door, and after going into the theatre, I sang a couple of arias for him. After leaving the stage I again found him waiting for me by the door, full of enthusiasm about my voice and its prospects. He suggested another meeting, and when I reminded him that I was catching the midnight train for Paris his disappointment was tangible. He told me that he was about to start a European tour, and asked me to contact him wherever and whenever I could.

My explanation of my indifference to de Sabata may seem strange, but I knew that it was not only my voice that he liked – and wanted. I was simply not prepared to allow myself to become involved with a man in his late sixties. He had the most beautiful face – that of a saint – but it was like wax, devoid of all colour. He looked frighteningly fragile and ill, and so I opted out. However, I still sometimes rather regret my decision.

Igor and I had arranged to meet the day after my arrival in Paris. Walking down the stairs of my hotel, I saw him in the foyer and realized that he had changed almost beyond recognition. Yet enough of him was left for my heart to start racing. The hell he had gone through was written on his face, as was the alcoholism he had mentioned in his letter. But beneath the surface, his old personality – the Igor I had loved and still loved – remained. This was enough for me to pin my hopes on a future together, and so I decided to marry and start a new life with him.

According to French law I was required to spend six weeks in Paris before being able to marry there, and so Igor and I spent a great deal of time together, recapturing the past. I realized that he was drinking a great deal but, never having been confronted so directly with alcoholism before, I had no idea what the problem would involve. I soon found out, and by the end of the six weeks I had realized the ghastly mistake I would be making by going ahead with the marriage. Yet something in my nature forbade me to throw in the towel. To have run away at this point would have left unfinished business, not to mention the possibility of being haunted for years to come by my memory of Igor – and possibly by he himself, in person. Deep down, I also still hoped that he would realize the golden possibilities of our joint life and throw himself into it. I was determined to give him, and us, a chance.

By now Gene had signed up an Italian opera company to appear at the Stoll Theatre in London in two months' time. I was to sing in *Tosca*, *La Forza del Destino* and *La Traviata*, and so, for the time being, my professional future was assured. I envisaged my career blossoming, Igor becoming my manager, and life opening up for both of us. We were married in the local *mairie* in Paris and soon afterwards left for London. But no sooner had we arrived than the troubles began.

Igor had never seen me in the role of the opera diva, and he resented my success. This made his drinking, which he had hither-to tried to hide from me, increase alarmingly. Furthermore, he would not admit his alcoholism and became aggressive at any men-tion of it. By now I was singing *Tosca* with Gobbi and Tagliavini and *La Forza del Destino* with Bergonzi, and I needed as much tranquillity and normality as possible. Yet I had bound myself to a completely amoral and egotistical alcoholic who passed over every opportunity that was presented to him – sometimes on a golden platter – in order to satisfy his addiction.

After our London season the Italian Opera Company went on a long tour, and for the first two weeks Igor accompanied me. But I found it very difficult to combine my busy schedule with trying to cope with his ever-increasing consumption of drink. Life became nerve-racking and very embarrassing, and although I did everything in my power to put a brave face on the situation, before long even this could not camouflage what was really happening. By now Igor had also started to show a very violent side that was always ready to explode, and after I had the shattering experience of being battered by him during the first interval of a performance of *Tosca*, I refused to allow him to come on tour with me any more. This was so sordid and appalling an affair, and I had no one to help me or to keep an eye on what was happening, and no one to whom I could pour out my grief.

After three months even I realized the inevitability of the end of our life together. The marriage was over, and I had no choice but to buy Igor a ticket back to Paris. However, I was so devastated by the thought of losing him that I rang the station master at Victoria Station, asking him to tannoy Igor's name for him to come to the telephone. I then abjectly begged him to return home, which he did. However, this made matters even worse, and eventually he had to leave London for good.

Of all my failures and traumas, my marriage to Igor was the worst and the hardest to accept; and it is hard to explain how I managed to live through this period and the subsequent realization that my chance of happiness had gone for ever. But I let Igor go, and eventually accepted the situation. However, I paid a great price. I knew I was on the verge of a breakdown, and I screamed for help.

I went to a doctor friend, George Sava (author of the famous *The Healing Knife*), who confirmed that I was on the brink of emotional collapse. He warned me that one of two things would happen: if I did nothing, and allowed myself to slip further down the slippery slope and over the edge, I might never recover; but if I could summon enough strength to acknowledge and face my predicament, I would have within me the power to survive it. He advised me to go away to new and convivial surroundings: Italy. I did as he suggested, going first to Milan and then on to Brescia, where several of my operatic colleagues were performing. I felt shaky, but the warmth and the excitement of the country enveloped and soothed me.

Soon after my arrival I went to a dress rehearsal of Tebaldi in *Tosca*. She sang superbly until the end of the rehearsal at eleven-thirty in the evening, but by midnight she had suddenly lost her voice completely. Knowing that I had recently sung the role with some of the artists who were to appear with her the following evening, the management rang me at my hotel and begged me to save the situation. However, the co-*répétiteur*, with whom I had worked a great deal in England and whose opinion was always of great importance to me, strictly forbade me to take part in the performance. He told me that Tebaldi was adored and worshipped in Brescia and that I, a foreigner, could be booed off the stage – if I did not suffer an even worse fate at the hands of the audience. This could end my career in Italy.

As much as I would have liked to take up the challenge, the various problems involved in this sudden crisis (including the fact that I had no costumes of my own, and would have had to wear makeshifts) all combined to create a risk that was too great for me to take. It could have made me; but it could also have finished me in one fell swoop. A substitute Tosca was found for each of the subsequent performances, but both singers were very mediocre. I was therefore both glad and sorry that I had chickened out.

If only fate had intervened, and Gene and I had parted much earlier, I think I could have built up a career in Italy and achieved great things. As it was, Gene was no longer living with me but he was still in my life, mostly when he was *not* needed and never when he *was*. And the two of us were still playing the old waiting game, the broom always ready to shoot. I think there is a real honour among thieves – for 'thieves' read 'managers and agents' – for, although I knew that I was very obviously admired for my looks and my voice, no one seemed to have the temerity to make a stand against Gene on my behalf. It was as if there were an invisible notice pinned on me that read PRIVATE PROPERTY – DO NOT TOUCH, and this was still strictly adhered to, even though the context had long ago lost its meaning.

Of course, there were opportunities, but my fear of peripheral involvement, and the dubious results these could have had, frightened me – and, I am sure, shut many a door that could have opened on to a veritable paradise. We so easily say, 'Nothing ventured, nothing gained'; and yet how can we tell which ventures are good and which are bad? Were we educated to make such choices, life would be a bowl of cherries.

23

Queen's Gate

B Y THE TIME of my reunion with Igor I had moved into a
ground floor flat in Queen's Gate. My fondest memory of that
area of London, apart from the bewitching Kensington Gardens
which were more or less on my doorstep, is of the almost unreal
atmosphere of Hyde Park Gate. It lay parallel, sandwiched between
Queen's Gate and Gloucester Road, a cul-de-sac except for an almost
hidden pathway winding into Gloucester Road. In the middle was a
rectangular garden locked behind beautiful iron railings. There was
a total silence and sense of exclusion about it, and the fact that I
never saw anyone use it made its isolation even more tantalizing.

On the left, in a huge Victorian house, lived Jacob Epstein, the
great sculptor, larger than life and often to be seen strolling down
towards Kensington Gardens. I would sometimes also see Lucien
Freud (his son-in-law) in the area; and because I have always been
awestruck by celebrities, such sightings invariably made my day.

On the right of Hyde Park Gate lived Winston Churchill, and on
one magic afternoon while I was taking a constitutional, my reverie
was suddenly interrupted by a sight that I will never forget: the
drawing-room in Churchill's house was brightly lit, with the cur-
tains open, and the great man was sitting in a huge armchair,
smoking an immense cigar. In the doorway, frozen in time for one
glorious moment, was Lady Churchill in profile – and was it exquisite! – holding a tea tray and about to enter the room. This was like
an image from a magic lantern of history, painted forever in my
mind – a split-second of still life, which I was there to capture.

✳

Another of my memories of Queen's Gate is of an incident that
would *never* happen today. One of the first Waitrose provisions
shops was on the corner of Queen's Gate Terrace and Gloucester
Road, and it was there that I used to do my shopping. On one
particular Saturday morning the order that I had placed by telephone was not delivered, and I phoned to complain bitterly that as
a result I was now minus a lunch. The manager of the shop suggested that I go, with a guest, to any restaurant in the vicinity, to
choose whatever I wish, and to charge the cost to Waitrose. This I
did – and that is what I call service!

✳

Soon after moving to Queen's Gate I went off to a BBC rehearsal of Spontini's *La Vestale*. Before my first vocal entry, there was some introductory singing by a 'High Priestess', sung by the Australian soprano Rosina Raisbeck. For some reason, she had rather serious vocal problems in the high passages and I found this puzzling, as they did not seem that difficult to me.

The moment I returned home, I rushed to the piano with the score of *La Vestale* and tried out the problem passages. They seemed easy enough, so I tried them again. As I did so, there was a thunderous banging on the ceiling that gathered force with the sound of my voice. When I stopped singing, the banging stopped. When I sang the phrase once more, the banging returned, even louder than before. Absolutely dumbfounded, I asked a friend who was staying with me to go up and investigate.

He returned very shaken, and told me that the door of the apartment upstairs had been opened by a man who said his wife was in a very distressed state. He had then asked him to come in and speak to her. The woman was indeed in a state of hysteria, screaming that she was Vera Schwarz (a singer in the early seasons at Glyndebourne, and well known before the Second World War) and that the gentleman who had opened the door to my friend was her husband, who had married her on condition that she give up her career. She had done so, and was now paying the price.

She could not cope with hearing any music whatsoever – not even a piano. As for a voice, that was totally unbearable. And, to add insult to injury, my voice was so like hers that she had nearly had a heart attack on hearing it. She could not stand this agony, and kept giving me an ultimatum: either I promise never to sing in my flat, or she would have to leave hers.

Within two weeks they had vacated their flat and disappeared out of my life. What a sad story.

24

Mary Garden

ONE OF MY MOST VALUED ENCOUNTERS with a 'Great' was an unexpected meeting with Mary Garden. In 1951 I was the soprano of the Italian Quartet touring Britain with enormous success (our star and tenor was Gino Mattera – the 'Armand' of the 1950s film of *La Traviata*). While we were performing in Aberdeen, I was just about to go out on stage to sing the aria from *Ernani* when someone rushed in to tell me that Mary Garden was in the audience.

My knees buckled and my voice rose to choke me as I suddenly recalled the Garden legend that she had left behind her in the United States. 'Unapproachable' ... 'Hates all other sopranos' ... 'Is hypercritical and bitchy' ... I gibbered to our manager that he would have to change the running order of appearances as I could not possibly go on until I had pulled myself together. But before I knew it, I was physically pushed on stage.

As I started singing, gazing as always into the distance at Circle level, I noticed Garden's silhouette in the very front row. She was sitting straight up, her lorgnette held firmly in her hand. I sang in a daze, and when I reached my dressing-room afterwards, Mary Garden had beaten me to it. She rushed at me with open arms, embraced me, and said, 'My dear, you belong to my generation. I didn't know there were any more left. You have what it takes to be a diva – not like that dreadful so-and-so' (mentioning one of the eminent 'Greats') 'who sang here recently. She has no right to be on the stage.'

She started asking me about my career, and was amazed at the difficulties confronting me. She promised to help me in any way she could. And I know that she did try to do so, writing to many people in Britain and in Italy on my behalf. But time was against her. The people that mattered had retired or died, or simply did not care. However, she gave me warmth and hospitality, and a new confidence in myself.

My next visit to Aberdeen was as Tosca, Mary Garden's great role. There was a note from her at the theatre, asking for a ticket and saying that she never thought she would actually want to see a Tosca – she never normally acknowledged other singers in that role. She was given a box in the theatre, and looked splendid. After the performance, she came backstage to congratulate me and presented me with her own 'Tosca' ring – the last of her 'props'.

I feel so sad now that I cannot remember more of our talks together, and I regret that I did not ask more questions about her career and about herself as a person. But I think that, in addition to my diffidence, and of course the enormous awe for someone older and so much greater than I, there was a rather cold reserve about her that I did not wish to encroach upon. Furthermore, distance and my peregrinations made contact with her difficult.

However, I can never forgive life for what it did to her in the end. She died alone in a mental home. There, but for the grace of God, go we.

25

Boris Christoff

In 1952 the great bass Christoff and I were jointly giving an important Royal Albert Hall concert conducted by Vilem Tausky. The rehearsal was scheduled at the Maida Vale Studios from two until five the previous afternoon, but unfortunately I was already rehearsing all that week – at the Camden Theatre, for an operetta broadcast conducted by Gilbert Vintner. I therefore passed a message to Christoff that he could rehearse from two until four p.m. and that I would then take over from four until five. This would leave him a whole two hours for rehearsal with the orchestra. He took this as a personal insult from me – how *dare* I be busy on the day of our rehearsal when *he* was available?

On the afternoon in question, Vilem Tausky and the orchestra arrived at the studios in readiness for Christoff. They waited and waited for him, but in vain. No Christoff. The members of the orchestra sighed, looked bored, read their newspapers, and did their crossword puzzles. At about three o'clock a sense of panic seized Christoff's agents and they rang the Savoy, where he was staying. There was no answer from his phone, and so they rushed over to the hotel to look for him. Getting no reply from his room, and learning that no one at the Savoy had seen or heard Christoff since that morning, they were forced to hang around the hotel, feeling increasingly desperate.

At exactly a quarter to four Christoff emerged from behind a massive pillar at the Savoy, where he had been lurking. He made for the front entrance and hailed a taxi, followed smartly by his agents. He arrived at Maida Vale at four o'clock precisely, just as I was getting out of my own cab. There was a slightly ominous confrontation between us, after which we all strode into the studios together. I took the lead and said, 'Mr Christoff, as you are a visitor to this country, you obviously have the prerogative; so please use the remaining hour still left to rehearse. I have no option but to forego my own rehearsal.' The orchestra awoke, put away their crossword puzzles, and started work. I, meanwhile, went home.

My programme for the concert was a formidable one. In addition to Tatyana's Letter Scene from *Eugene Onegin* and Jaroslavna's Lament from *Prince Igor*, both of which I had often performed, it included the Swan-Princess aria from *Tsar Sultan* and Ludmilla's Cavatina from *Russlan and Ludmilla*, neither of which I had ever sung before. With no orchestral rehearsal, this was not a pleasant prospect for a young, aspiring singer.

Looking back, I find it amusing to recall that when I met both Christoff and Tagliavini socially in Italy – Christoff in the offices of the Teatro Reale in Rome, and Tagliavini at his own dress rehearsal of *Tosca* at La Scala, to which he himself had invited me – they were charm itself, like dogs with three tails. It was only when I became a colleague (which they interpreted as a *competitor*) that their childish obstinacy and insecurity rose to the fore.

*

Another enchanting incident involving Christoff occurred at the Royal Opera House, Covent Garden, on the occasion of a dress rehearsal of *Boris Godunov*. Something peeved him in mid-flow, and he simply stomped off the stage and disappeared. After waiting quite some time for him to return, it was decided to send out a search party.

The theatre was toothcombed, and every nook and cranny searched. But no Christoff. Having lost his patience, the conductor rather peremptorily decided that the rehearsal would continue regardless, and gave instructions for Marian Novakowski, Christoff's understudy, to be called. When this message was relayed over the tannoy, Christoff suddenly flushed himself out of the ladies' WC – the one place that no one had thought of looking for him – and arrived on stage together with Novakowski.

26

The Hornets' Nest

AFTER THE FAILURE of my disastrous marriage in 1952, I went to Milan in search of a career. One day at a theatre, I was waiting at the box office to buy a ticket for that evening's performance when I suddenly heard Russian being spoken in front of me. This beguiling sound seduced me, as always, into introducing myself in Russian to the speaker, and contact was immediate. She was a pleasant lady of an uncertain age who expressed her delight at meeting me, and after we had chatted for a while we exchanged phone numbers.

The next day, she rang me to say that Russian friends of hers were interested in meeting me, and asked if I would be their guest at a restaurant the following evening. I accepted the invitation and duly arrived at the venue, joining a party of about twelve women – all Russian and all of a similarly uncertain age. I found this situation rather bizarre, and soon noticed that at the head of the table sat the hostess, an elegant *belle femme*, whom everyone treated with a certain deference. She had been a ballerina, and was married to the proprietor of a large and successful chain of shops – the equivalent of Mothercare – all over Italy.

Picking up snippets of conversation, I realized that this was a sort of unofficial club, and it became clear to me that the women were not only of an uncertain age but also of an uncertain sexuality – as indeed was the hostess's husband. This was something quite outside my social precinct and beyond both my understanding and my personal acceptance, and yet I was rather amused to find myself inadvertently in the midst of it. I was amazed to discover that another Russian whom they knew was Daria Bayan, my colleague in *The Fair of Sorochintsi* ten years earlier. When Jay Pomeroy finally had his comeuppance and was indicted for owing vast amounts of unpaid income tax, Bayan had quickly slipped out of London and landed in Milan, together with a few valuables including a Tintoretto or two. She was now ensconced in the grand Hotel Continentale, almost adjoining La Scala, and the legend went that she spoke of her voice as being so superb that she hesitated to let anyone hear it, in case she caused embarrassment to other great singers who would simply give up their careers in despair.

The dinner at an end, we all went our separate ways with an *arrivederci a presto*, and as far as I was concerned, this was purely perfunctory because I had no intention of becoming involved with them in any way. But a couple of days later, my Russian friend rang me again and invited me to a large party being given by one of the coterie. I apologized and said that I was otherwise engaged. The next day she phoned me to say how sorry they all were at my absence, adding that the evening had been a riot – a brilliant trans-vestite celebration. I was doubly glad that I had not accepted the invitation, but this was not, as I had expected, the end of the story.

Before coming to Milan I had been given an introduction to the British Council representative in Rome, whose name was John Graham. When I rang him to make contact, he invited me to din-ner, adding joyfully that he would also be inviting someone I would be delighted to meet again: Daria Bayan. There was no way that I could back out, but when I arrived he told me sadly that poor Daria had suddenly developed a bad migraine and sent her apologies. I tactfully remarked that I was familiar with her headaches, and sounded most sympathetic.

One day, while I was alone at a cinema, I heard an announce-ment over the tannoy: '*La Signora Vayne è chiamata al telefono – per favore.*' This was repeated several times before I realized that it was meant for me. Panic-stricken, I rushed to the manager's office to find myself on the receiving end of a telephone call from ALCI, the number one operatic agency in Italy. Would I come immediately to their offices to sing for Commendatore Siciliani, director of the Florence Opera House?

In a daze, I rushed to my hotel, picked up some music, and arrived at the offices to find various important people waiting for me. I sang several arias and Siciliani was more than enthusiastic. 'This will be a cannon shot' (*un Colpo di Cannone*), he said, 'and will prove to Callas and Tebaldi that they are not irreplaceable, now that they are too big to sing for us.' He immediately offered me the role of Donna Anna in Dargomijsky's opera *The Stone Guest*, add-ing that the directors fully realized that the role would not do jus-tice to my range or voice; however, they would use this as a springboard, leading to far greater things. I believed them, and signed the contract there and then.

Through the grapevine I had heard that Daria Bayan was being promoted by the 'dykes co-operative' to make a sensational début in an opera to be mounted in Florence. So, when I unexpectedly signed for *The Stone Guest*, I realized that I had pipped her at the post. As my situation was now hotting up, I was delighted to be leaving Milan. However, I soon discovered that the opera's director, Tatyana Pavlova, was one of the most powerful and dangerous leaders of the pack. She had escaped from Russia in 1917 at about the same time as Eugene Iskoldoff (they had been colleagues together) and arrived in Italy, where she became a very highly renowned actress, comparable to the great Duse.

Pavlova had led an extremely hectic life, and having aged badly and lost her ability to charm the men, she decided to try her luck with women. Her attitude to non-compliant ladies, such as I, was lethal – and I really mean that. She did what she could to ruin my sojourn in Florence – and with it my Italian début. Luckily, she did not succeed. But this was only by a fluke, for she always drove at least one member of the company she was directing to resign in tears. This happened to us, and our co-*répétiteur* – a charming and talented young man – left the company in great distress.

Eventually Daria Bayan could no longer hold back her divine voice, and she had no choice but to air it publicly. She gave a recital and died a rather exposed death. Where *was* that miraculous voice, the instrument that would put all other singers, however great, to shame?

27

The Stone Guest

WHILE WE WERE IN REHEARSAL for *The Stone Guest* in 1953, rumours reached us of a phenomenal soprano, newly arrived from the United States. She was allegedly so extraordinary that rehearsals for the forthcoming production of *Agnese di Hohenstaufen* were being held behind locked doors – no one was allowed to hear her before her stupendous début. However, a few of us somehow managed to sneak into the auditorium where she was rehearsing, and we heard this 'phenomenon'.

She was over six feet tall, clumsy, completely myopic, and obviously without any stage experience whatsoever. Her voice was fairly pedestrian and had nothing to set it apart from many other, equally basic, voices. However, the explanation that wafted down the grapevine made it all very clear: she had won an important voice competition run by one of the largest petroleum companies in the USA, and was being financed by them!

The première of *The Stone Guest* was a great success. My 'crits' were brilliant – one of them saying, in effect, that I had 'out-Callassed' Callas, both vocally and histrionically. But although I had had no contact with the press, my colleagues – naturally – accused me of bribery! When our performances came to an end, the 'phenomenal' soprano, by the name of Lucilla Udovic, made her début. The reception was tepid, and her subsequent début at Glyndebourne as Elettra in *Idomeneo* was not received any more enthusiastically. For myself, however, that promise of greater things never materialized. Miss Udovic had got there first – with, alas, so little to show for it. But I became reasonably friendly with her. She was pleasant and very naïve, taking for granted the prize that had fallen into her lap and considering herself on a far higher plane than I. It seems that she later sustained a career of sorts, singing a wide repertoire but without ever leaving a great impression on the operatic world.

Around forty years later, a friend of mine in Rome came across a recording of *The Stone Guest*, pirated from a broadcast by CETRA and RAI (the Italian equivalent of the BBC), in a flea market. I had completely forgotten the music – and almost everything about the production – but when my friend sent me a tape of the recording I was astonished by the quality of my voice and kept looking at the label to make sure it was really me! My voice must have been at the peak of its form when the recording was made. Listening objectively, as I always do, I once again marvelled at the tricks that fate played on me.

A wave of other memories of *The Stone Guest* also came over me. The conductor was to have been Issay Dobrowen, and after a few days of piano rehearsals he decided to hear a run-through of the complete First Act. For reasons known only to himself, he then 'protested' – another word for scrapped – the entire company. I was the only exception, because my role of Donna Anna has only one short phrase right at the end of the act. The directors conferred and decided that, rather than having to recast the entire opera, it would be better to pay off Dobrowen and then engage a new conductor. The new maestro was Emidio Thierry.

For reasons unknown to us, a famous mezzo in the company was sacked and replaced by the Serb mezzo, Marianna Radev. This shook the rest of the cast and made them feel very insecure, and while chatting to the tenor, Fausto Flammini, who was singing the role of Don Juan, I realized that he was quite panic-stricken. He had a lovely, if slightly rough, voice, but his musicianship was nil. I felt so sorry for him that I suggested helping him in the only way I could: we spent about three hours together, in which I marked every crotchet, quaver, and minim in the score with its relevant value. This had so often worked for me, and it worked for him. I gave him back his confidence, and as this was his first ever stage role, its importance was immeasurable. Alas, although he sang well and looked great, I do not think he ever had a follow-up engagement.

After Florence I did not return to Milan but went to Rome, and almost immediately auditioned for the Teatro del Opera. The following Saturday afternoon, I received a telephone call asking me whether I could undertake the role of Aida at the famous Caracalla Baths – the scheduled soprano was ill. Although I knew the part, I had never sung it, and after thinking quickly I wisely refused the offer, knowing that without even a cursory rehearsal it might be a dreadful disaster because of the enormous cast, the totally unfamiliar sets, and the odd horse or elephant to contend with.

Everyone I spoke to in Rome gave me the same piece of advice: that without coaching from Luigi Ricci, a singer would find the doors of most Italian opera houses firmly closed. I therefore rang him and asked for an appointment, but he replied, 'Signora, I am very busy. Please call me again, perhaps in six months.' When, some time later, I was asked to take over 'Tosca' from Tebaldi, I was told that I must first be coached in the role by Ricci. When I rang him again, he said, 'Certainly, Signora. Tomorrow?'

By then I knew that he was on the board of the Opera House, and also that he was a tremendous womanizer. In view of my reaction to men of this sort, I feared that this chance, too, would be lost to me. However, as I entered his studio, he looked me up and down lingeringly, muttered, *'Che bel corpo'* (what a beautiful body), and, to my relief, left it at that.

At the time, I was working on my repertoire with his nephew, Mario Ricci, who was a superb coach. He was appalled to learn that I had an appointment with his uncle, and said, 'Signora, my uncle will murder your voice! His methods are disastrous! Come to me immediately after your session with him, and I will put right all the harm he will do to your voice.' This is what I did, with excellent results.

His uncle's methods were certainly bizarre. One had to stand in a corner of the room, face the wall, hold a book to each ear while pushing them forwards and bawl one's guts out, listening to the ghastly amplification thus produced. I soon evolved a compromise so that the effects were not as disastrous as they might have been. But Luigi Ricci was a very powerful man – one wrong step, and you were *out*!

To return to *The Stone Guest* for a moment, I recall another incident, which throws light on much of the operatic profession. A young baritone, who shall remain nameless, had a walk-on part in the production, and we became buddies. He talked of his enormous ambitions, and always reiterated that he would stop at nothing to make a career. He certainly stuck to his vow until he had reached his goal.

During the period of *The Stone Guest* he had become a protégé of Commendatore Siciliani, whose private passions were male-orientated, and when I met him in Rome a very short time afterwards he informed me that he was about to sing 'Scarpia' in an important Stagione. He admitted that he was terrified at the prospect, for this would be, almost literally, his first role on stage. He also became close to the dreaded accompanist Favaretto, without whom one could hardly make a professional move in Italy. Very soon this baritone was singing at the Met in New York and forging an international reputation. He certainly had the talent, but would he have travelled the long road to fame quite so quickly with different principles?

28

Rome – Hopes and Disappointments

ROME SEEMED so different from Milan – much more welcoming and generous – and when I arrived there, my hopes were high. In addition to contacting the city's Teatro Reale, I had written to the San Carlo Opera in Naples, and I soon received their reply, giving me an audition date. The director, an attractive, youthful man, listened to me with Maestro Vincenzo Bellezza, a very prestigious conductor, and my audition was a great success. It was suggested that in the following season I would take over the title role in *Adriana Lecouvreur* from Maria Caniglia, and I was told to return to Rome to await a summons from Naples.

Time passed, and with no further communication from the San Carlo, I contacted them. I was asked to audition again, which I did – with similar success. Bellezza was not present for this second audition, but the young director was charm itself; he informed me that I was top of their list of *prima donnas*, and that confirmation of my engagement would be sent to me in Rome within a few days' time. However, a further long silence ensued, so once more I contacted them. And once more I was asked to audition. The by now familiar scenario was repeated: I sang for the charming director who then said, 'Signora, you are top of the list. Don't worry, we will contact you very shortly. *Pazienza!*' There was silence yet again, but this time I decided that enough was enough.

Soon afterwards I ran into Maestro Bellezza in Rome, and he politely asked me if I would be singing Adriana in the forthcoming production that he was going to conduct. When I recounted the sequence of events at the San Carlo he looked concerned and asked, 'Did they ask you for money, or did they offer you a hotel room?' Amazed, I stammered, 'No Maestro, they did neither. Please believe me.' He smiled sardonically and explained, 'They certainly asked you. You simply did not understand.'

He then mentioned a very well-known singer who, on a different occasion, had obviously understood the body language of the San Carlo director for whom she auditioned: she signed a contract after accepting the hotel room – thereby consenting to make herself available in it as and when necessary. I realized that I should have had an 'interpreter' in Naples with me, as I had failed to read

between the lines and had completely missed the inference of the
director's words of promise.

Here I must add that, by all accounts, Bellezza was a man of
great integrity. He certainly never propositioned me in any way
whatsoever. But another of my professional dreams had been
snuffed out. All that came of my three trips to Naples was an
invitation from the accompanist in residence to inaugurate the first
ever vocal recital on the island of Ischia (by then the home of Sir
William Walton). He saw in me a recitalist's potential – something
not always present in Italian singers.

The invitation to sing Tosca at the Teatro Reale in Rome was, in
fact, a gesture of compensation towards me. Having heard me sing,
the management asked me to study *Fedora*, a production of which
was to be mounted in the coming season. No contract was signed,
the word of a gentleman being sufficient guarantee for me, and I
returned to England to fulfil engagements and to study *Fedora*
there. Shortly after going back to Rome, fully prepared to make my
début, I bumped into Maestro Bellezza again – it must have been
providence. When I joyfully told him that I had returned to sing
Fedora for the Teatro Reale, his face once more took on a look of
deep concern. He told me that there had been a change of government in Italy and that the previous plans had had to be scrapped in
favour of the latest opera by Pizzetti, who had enormous clout with
the new government. Bellezza looked as if he could weep for me.

＊

In Italy I was obviously recognized as a singer-actress, and looking
back, I *should* have been able to create a special niche for myself.
During this period I had the pleasure of singing Tosca in Genoa
with the great baritone Antenore Reale. He was then quite elderly
and at the end of his career, but his Scarpia was outstanding. I also
had the privilege of singing Santuzza in *Cavalleria Rusticana* with
the greatest tenor of them all, Beniamino Gigli, in his home town
of Recanati – which is in fact two towns, one high on a hill and
surrounded by a wall, the other below on the shores of the Adriatic.
The occasion was both Gigli's last operatic appearance and the for-
tieth anniversary of his début, and he was singing in both
Cavalleria and *I Pagliacci*.

As always, there was not even a run-through, and interpreting
my role very emotionally, I threw myself at him in our scene together, only to hear him hiss, '*Non toccarmi, non toccarmi!*' (Do not
touch me). I realized at once that he had to conserve all his energies
in order to perform both of these gruelling roles, and I therefore

kept my emotional outbursts to myself. Acting had never been a strong point of Gigli's, but with a voice like his, who needs histrionics?

✳

It has always astonished me how little, if at all, the British powers-that-be abroad have helped aspiring artists who have dared to leave their own shores, particularly when a little encouragement and support could open so many doors. I had had an introduction to John Graham of the British Council in Milan, but all he could do was to set the ball rolling. The outcome was a dinner party with the consul and his wife, at which, during one of those pregnant social silences, she turned to me and said very patronizingly, 'I hear you are going to be singing in *Tosca*.' I replied that indeed I was, to which she asked, 'And what role will you be singing?' Managing to stifle a smirk, I muttered, 'Oh, the Shepherd Boy...' Needless to say, the consul and his wife always had a box at La Scala at their disposal!

I later attended a more public dinner, given in Milan in my honour, at which I was to sing. At the latter event I was introduced, by a greatly inebriated master of ceremonies, as 'Vera Kane, just arrived from Tuscany' – presumably he meant *Tosca*!

Soon afterwards John Graham moved to Rome and again, he did what he could for me by giving me a recital at the British Council's wonderful palace in the Via delle Quattro Fontane. The audience was fairly sparse and rather inauspicious, and after the recital John apologized over a sherry for the meagre attendance and refreshments, saying that, logically, my recital should have been given at the British Embassy on a far grander scale. However, the ambassador, Sir Ashley Clarke, was himself an amateur pianist who loved to give concerts, and when organizing musical events he promoted himself rather than other, more deserving, performers. The entertainment after his own recitals was apparently lavish beyond imagination.

Sure enough, I soon received an invitation to a four-hand piano recital that Sir Ashley was giving with another amateur pianist. The magnificent concert hall was filled to capacity, yet the boredom on everyone's faces was almost tangible. The reception afterwards was indeed of bacchanalian proportions: lashings of caviar and smoked salmon, and champagne in abundance.

There were quite a few British vocal students in Rome, trying to eke out an existence on a weekly grant of five pounds and therefore having to work full-time at whatever they could while studying only peripherally in the evenings. Only one amongst them made a career, and that was Anna Reynolds; but she obviously had other means of surviving. It so happened that I was the first British singer after Eva Turner to have arrived in post-war Italy fully trained and ready for the big professional breaks; so it should not have been too difficult for the Embassy to give me a helping hand in some way.

The Embassy and Sir Ashley were of course notified of my *Tosca* début, and it should have been a *fait accompli* to give a small reception in my honour following the performance. After all, it was not every day that a Brit sang at the Teatro Reale and followed Tebaldi – not the easiest act in Italy to follow, either. Instead, I received an odd note from Sir Ashley explaining regretfully that neither he nor any representative had managed to make the performance, and that they had tried all day to phone the box office – without any success. One would have had to be extremely gullible to accept such an excuse, especially as the ambassador always had a box at his disposal. He added that he hoped his flowers had reached me safely and gave me pleasure. There were compensations, however, including a guaranteed invitation to the Queen's birthday party!

In contrast, the American Embassy did whatever it could to back as many of its own aspiring artists as possible, providing, among other comforts, the use of a lovely hostel at minimal charges. At that time, American singers arriving in Italy (sometimes with their agents) quickly realized that instead of auditioning ad lib and waiting for their big chance to arrive, it was far quicker and easier to *buy* a performance and thus, in one fell swoop, present themselves in a leading role. As most of the singers were very talented, this was a wonderful way to make a name for themselves.

Another important factor was that they were all competition winners, whereas in England at that time there were no such contests for singers whatsoever. With such a marked difference of approach between the two countries, it is not surprising that so many young American vocalists made immediate and important careers.

On reflection, however, the most significant factor in my own lack of continuing success in Italy was this: it was an acknowledged fact that, as a foreigner, I should have gone through the necessary 'motions', when receiving my honorarium, of retaining the envelope but returning the cash inside it to the powers-that-be – either that or presenting them with an expensive present, of a similar value to my fee – in order to express my 'gratitude' to them. I was advised by my Italian colleagues, time and time again, to do this, and the reasons why I never complied with this tradition were

1. Mother (first from left),
   Moscow, *c.* 1898.

2. Mother. Moscow, *c.* 1900.

3. My half-sisters Alice and
   Vera. St Petersburg, *c.* 1908.

4. Maya. St Petersburg, 1915.

5. My 'last' photo; holding a rusk and sitting next to my sister Maya (right). Anapa, 1919.

6. Father, 1917.

7. Kyra, south London, 1925.

8. As Bonnie Prince Charlie.
   Glasgow, 1941.

9. My first press release photo, mid-1940s.

10. With Eugene Iskoldoff on the RMS *Queen Mary* sailing to New York, 1948.

11. Kyra arriving in Hollywood, 1949 with Eugene Iskoldoff (left) and actor Ivan Lebedoff (right).

12. As Tosca. The Stoll Theatre, London, 1952.

13. Rome, 1954.

14. Preparing for a performance of *The Stone Guest*. Florence, 1953.

15. As Tosca (Act One). The Stoll Theatre, 1952.

16. As Santuzza with Gigli after his final operatic performance: *Cavalleria Rusticana*. Rome, August 1954.

17. With Virginia Zeani. Aberdeen, 1953.

18. As Tatyana in *Eugene Onegin*, with Carl-Axel Hallgren. Aarhus, Denmark, 1958.

19. An early portrait, *c.* 1937: wearing the bracelet given to me by Princess Andrew of Russia.

20. Sixty years on; at home in West Kensington, 1997.

twofold. Firstly, I did not wish to line the pockets of those in charge, particularly as what I had to sell to them was worth every lira. Secondly, and more prosaically, I needed that money in order to eat!

This is the simple explanation why, when my reviews were excellent and my personal success enormous, I was never offered return dates. As a result, my career in Italy never lived up to my potential.

29

Tosca

A s TOSCA was the role most closely associated with me, and as singing it appeared to be a catalyst for various unexpected disasters or humorous incidents, it deserves a chapter of its own.

The first incident was at my début with the Italian Opera Company in the wonderful old Stoll Theatre in Holborn, built especially for opera by Sir Oswald Stoll and, alas, demolished in the early 1960s. Apart from myself, the entire company was Italian and included such greats as Gobbi, Tagliavini, Gianni Raimondi, Bergonzi, Zamphigi, Tagliabue, Carosio, Magda Olivero and Virginia Zeani. *Tosca* being a repertory opera, there were no rehearsals as such. Gobbi and I had a frosty piano run-through (with Tagliavini there was not even this most elementary of musical rehearsals) during which I received my first initiation into the business of prompting, without which no Italian singer would dream of performing.

A prompter, or *soggeritore*, does more than simply remind singers of words when they forget them; he cues *every* vocal entry in slight anticipation of the beat. As a result, one is conscious of a distinct syncopation that can be very unsettling until one has adjusted to it. The situation in England at that time was very different: with perhaps the exception of Covent Garden, it was not customary to have a prompter, and this was certainly the first time that I had ever worked with one. I realized very quickly that I had to adjust to this new method of performing, but I was amazed that Gobbi, who must have sung Scarpia a hundred or more times, was so used to performing with the assistance of a *soggeritore* that he could not manage without one.

For my entrance in the Second Act and the big *scena* with Scarpia, I wore a beautiful white and gold Regency gown (designed by Michael Whittaker, then a very fashionable film and theatre designer) with a *décolletage* edged with ostrich feathers. As Scarpia, Gobbi was in full histrionic steam – the villain proper, ruthless in his destruction of Tosca – and although he was savagely giving his all when facing the audience, he turned his back on them when not singing. He then mimed orders to me and belittled me as I sang by forcing me, with his famous hypnotic gaze, into acquiescence.

Although I had studied the role of Tosca with Maria Kouznetzova in Paris and with Dennis Arundel and Powell Lloyd in London, and knew every possible dramatic option, Gobbi made a puppet out of me. And in the seduction scene he really went to town.

Having had no stage rehearsal whatsoever with him, I was totally unprepared for his brutality and had not been able to gauge how dangerous my ostrich feather collar was in the circumstances: he shook me very powerfully until I was literally gasping for breath, and during one of these gasps I inhaled one of the feathers. This was immediately before my aria 'Vissi d'arte', which I was forced to sing sprawled on the ground where Gobbi had flung me. 'Vissi d'arte' has no orchestral introduction at all, merely a lead note before the aria begins, and my first few notes were a stifled gurgle. Then, the feather having mercifully cleared from my larynx, I continued the aria successfully.

In the audience that night were many important and influential people such as Princess Marina and David Webster (the then director of Covent Garden), in addition to reporters and music critics. At the end of the Act, I rushed to our public relations officer and asked her to inform the media of what had happened to me. She refused to do so, saying, 'It's not our policy. The least said the better.' Once again I resisted making demands to which I was more than entitled, but the result was that the media and everybody else present assumed that my lapse had resulted from first-night nerves, something that I never in fact suffered from.

My reviews the following day were rather tepid, and I found this very hard to live down. Ironically, there were huge newspaper headlines that same morning announcing 'Covent Garden Tenor Swallows His Moustache' – this happened to Walter Midgley during 'La donna è mobile' in *Rigoletto* on the same evening that I had swallowed my ostrich feather. Good for him that Covent Garden's policy differed from ours . . .

✳

My experience with Tagliavini was even worse. He had touted all the Italian restaurants in Soho, handing out tickets for the upper circle to his prospective 'supporters' in lieu of the traditional Italian claque – the organization of professional 'clappers' or applauders. When, during the performance of the opera, the recipients of these free gifts showed their appreciation not only for Tagliavini but also for *me*, his fury knew no bounds. In my Second Act aria he stood at the side of the stage and yelled, 'If she sings an encore, there will be no Third Act!' We all knew that he meant what he said, and any chance of an encore was immediately scuppered, especially as our conductor had already been tipped off.

At the end of the opera a flunkey appeared with flowers for me, at which point Tagliavini bawled, 'We, Tagliavini, do not allow flowers.' The flunkey tried to brush him aside, but the tenor leapt on him and clung on like a limpet. The curtain heaved to and fro, much to the audience's horror, and when we eventually slunk through it to take our bows, all the cast were crunching underfoot the flowers that had been strewn on the ground during the fracas.

I had the pleasure of singing Tosca with Tagliavini in Italy on several occasions, but the pattern of his behaviour was always the same: no encore and no flowers. At the Teatro Reale in Rome he had filled the circle with his usual paid claques and was incensed to find that the stalls audience did not, as usual, sit on their hands but befriended me and applauded me wildly, screaming, 'Encore! Encore!' Once again, the conductor had evidently been primed before the performance and tried several times to continue the scene, but he was forced to wait until the clamour had subsided. He then carried on regardless, allowing me no encore.

Tagliavini's home town was Piacenza, and when I sang Tosca there with him he was completely confident of his audience's adulation. After Cavaradossi's passionate outburst in the Third Act, Tosca replies with a few bars of sensuous lyricism, and I chose to sing these as softly and as tenderly as possible, in a mere whisper of voice. Afterwards there was a storm of applause – at a most unexpected point in the opera – and Tagliavini was once again enraged by my popularity with 'his' audience. He threw me across his knee, kissed me on the mouth, smearing my lipstick all over my face, and then, while holding me firmly with his right hand, deftly undid all the hooks and eyes down the back of my dress with his left hand. Having hurled my cloak at the villain Spoletta, I was therefore left to end the opera clutching the back of my dress while I threw myself into the River Arno.

There had been other problems with the production in Piacenza before opening night. Little Maestro Bottino, who had been co-répétiteur with the Italian Opera, was there again in the same capacity, as was our entire chorus. Bottino and I had a very good relationship, and I tried to ignore his private life which was anything but acceptable to me. He had a delightful Sardinian wife with blonde hair and blue eyes (a hybrid colouring resulting from the Austrian invasion) who sang in our chorus, *and* he had a pretty girlfriend – who also sang in the chorus – whom he openly flaunted whenever and wherever he could. In fact he was the randiest little bastard I would ever care to meet.

On that particular day, I had an appointment for a piano run-through with the conductor. If I proved to be inadequate, his would be the prerogative to 'protest' me, leaving my contract null and void. The rehearsal was at three p.m., and Bottino suggested that we have lunch together at my favourite trattoria, to which I agreed. When I arrived I was shattered to find the entire chorus there, including the girlfriend but *excluding* the wife. I realized at once that I was being used as a 'protection front' for Bottino and the girlfriend. Not wishing to make a scene, I remained in the restaurant and ordered lunch.

Halfway through the meal, the door flew open and Bottino's wife rushed in with a man, pointed at the girlfriend, and left. Relieved that she had gone, I continued my lunch. But the door burst open again, the wife flew towards the girlfriend, and, in a flash, the talons of her right hand ripped down the girl's face, leaving four ghastly, bleeding weals and defacing her beyond recognition. If there is one thing I cannot stand, it is the sight of blood – I can easily pass out or be violently sick. This was Latin revenge in the raw! During the ensuing chaos I realized that I was already late for my appointment, so I staggered out of the restaurant and into a taxi. Arriving at the studio, I managed to excuse my tardiness, pulled myself together, and somehow passed my test with flying colours.

That night was Franco Corelli's début in *Carmen*. He was stunning, vocally and visually, and it was obvious that he had a great career before him. Halfway through the performance, heavy snow started to fall, and by midnight it was waist-high. All the traffic had come to a dead stop, and tunnels had been cut through the snow for pedestrians. Nothing like this had ever happened in the region before. I was dressed in a black velvet evening coat, with very open, high-heeled sandals on my feet. There was no choice: somehow I had to make my way back to the hotel, frozen, soaking, slipping and slithering in my three-inch heels. I made it, and to my astonishment I was none the worse for wear the next day, which was the day of my début.

*

It was at the Teatro Reale in Rome that I had the first of my own direct encounters with the claque. Ten minutes before the curtain went up, there was a knock at my dressing-room door, and when I opened it I saw a smart gentleman who bowed low and asked how much I was prepared to pay him. To my question, 'Pay you for what?', he introduced himself as the chief claqueur and the representative of the others on duty. He explained that they would express their delight in my singing that evening in proportion to the amount of cash I gave him. Having spent many an evening in the upper circle of various Italian opera houses, in the thick of the claque gangs, I knew how the system operated, and I had often worked myself into a froth claquing for an artist I felt to be more deserving than the highest payer.

I made it clear to him that in no way would I contribute a single lira, as it was important for me to know my own worth without their help. He then rather menacingly replied that I would die an inevitable death on stage, for in no way could I hope to survive in Italy without the support of the claques. I told him that I would take that risk, and he left, his face suffused with anger.

My Scarpia at the Teatro Reale was Gian Giacomo Guelfi, a very popular baritone, and I was nervous about how he would treat me as, again, I had not even had a piano run-through with him. By a fluke, his wife had been a member of our opera chorus, and so I swallowed my pride and begged her to ask her husband not to jeopardize my performance. She was a very sweet person, and I think she realized how much the evening meant to me. Shortly afterwards, Guelfi came to me and assured me that he would do everything in his power to align his interpretation with mine. This made up for everything else and, my confidence restored, I was a big success with the audience.

✳

During a performance of *Tosca* at the Stoll Theatre, Antonio Manca Serra had taken over from Gobbi as Scarpia. He was a young man, small in stature and rather pigeon-chested, but with a sensuous, nostril-flaring, Mediterranean face and a fine acting technique. He looked gorgeous in his gold-embroidered black velvet costume and white wig, and it was a joy to work with him.

After I had 'killed' him in the Second Act he fell Centre Stage, his face towards the footlights and legs upstage, and I placed a lit candle on either side of his body. I then backed away in order to lift the crucifix off the wall and give him the 'last rites', so to speak. But I found that, instead of being the usual three to four inches long, the crucifix was twice that length. This threw me, and I slowed up slightly. Since every action had to be timed to the music I was now forced to hurry, and instead of gently laying the crucifix on his body, I threw it in time to the drum roll from the orchestra pit. Unfortunately it hit Antonio where it hurt most, and I was appalled to see him jerk his legs in the air before subsiding, with a twitch and a smirk, back into a corpse!

Tragically, Antonio died of a heart attack while singing in *Tosca* in Dublin soon after our season in London. He was only in his late thirties, and a superb artist.

✱

During a season with the Welsh National Opera as Tosca, my baritone was a well-known Sadlers Wells singer and a professional of long standing. On a previous occasion, with the Dublin Opera in *La Forza del Destino*, he had made a serious pass at me, which I politely refused. That he was incensed was obvious, but that he would harbour his rage until *now* seemed inconceivable. However . . .

The gown I was wearing in Act Two was of black velvet with a magnificent palantine, also of black velvet, lined and edged to the floor with simulated ermine. On my entrance 'Scarpia' should have greeted me and, with a broad gesture, swept the palantine off my shoulders and laid it across a chair. Instead, finding this a good moment for revenge, he greeted me and left me to dispose of the palantine myself. There was not a moment to lose, and with a strong jerk of my shoulders, I let the palantine slide off my back onto the floor. He had no choice but to bend down, grovelling, and pick it up. This in no way endeared me to him.

Because he had not been avenged, he lunged at me later in the Act, immediately after 'Vissi d'arte'. In a flash, and with his back to the audience, he undid my zip, which was almost the full length of the gown. I therefore had to 'murder' him, and go through all the many stage motions before the drop of the curtain, clutching my dress tightly at the back with my left hand and manipulating everything else – knife, candlesticks, and crucifix – with my right hand, making sure never to even half-turn my back. For, apart from a pair of briefs, I was nude under the gown. I even made my exit by backing to the door and kicking my train as it swirled itself into knots around my feet. One wonders what would have happened had my expertise at 'manipulation' been a little less expert . . . As the trick he played on me was the same as Tagliavini's in Piacenza, it seems as if this must be a ploy used by the vocal brotherhood in full blood!

During another performance in Cardiff, while Scarpia (sung by Roderick Jones) was singing after having finished his supper in Act Two, I noticed with dismay that the candles so essential to the end of the Act were unlit. I somehow managed to mime this information to Roderick, who very cleverly sauntered to the side of the stage while not singing, made signs to someone, and sauntered back with a box of matches hidden in his ample cuffs. He then very nonchalantly lit the candles with his back to the audience, and I was able to go through the necessary motions of placing a candlestick on either side of his body after he had 'died'.

On yet another occasion, when grasping what should have been a normal dinner knife with which to stab Scarpia, I found myself clutching a minute fruit knife, the only available instrument of death. This being totally useless, I was forced to camouflage my gestures, and in the end it must have seemed as if I stabbed him to death with my finger. When we came offstage I fumed to the props manager about the disaster, and he assured me that the same mistake would not happen the following night. And he was right: as I approached the table to pick up the knife, I found myself faced with a choice of every possible implement, from our old friend the fruit knife to a butcher's knife and a fourteenth-century dagger!

30

More Mishaps and Laughs

IN 1954 the Italian Opera Company was on tour, and my tenor in *La Traviata* was Fernando Bandera. He had a habit of using his heels, instead of the balls of his feet, to balance his body, and continued in his own obstinate, tenorial way no matter how often I warned him of the disasters to come. One day, as I was 'painfully' getting out of my bed in the Fourth Act, ready for his embrace, he rushed in – on his heels – and immediately started teetering backwards. I leapt up to him to try to prevent his backward fall, and as he straightened up we collided with a bump and collapsed in a heap, Centre Stage!

From the audience there was total silence for what seemed like several minutes. Then, as I tried to extricate myself, I started to laugh. And laugh. And laugh. Little by little, the audience joined in with me, and we all laughed until we could laugh no more. The conductor, David Ellenberg, an earnest young man with a bald pate but great tufts of curly black hair on either side of his head, drew himself up to his full height, put on his most prim expression, and, pointing his baton at poor 'Alfredo', waved him imperiously offstage.

Bandera did a quick turnaround and reappeared immediately, still running on his heels but with slightly less speed, and we started the sequence again.

✳

On one of our last tours, a new 'Azucena' joined us for *Il Trovatore*. She was in her mid-thirties, with a gorgeous mezzo voice, but otherwise she had little to recommend her. With no stage experience, clumsily built, and completely cross-eyed, her only other asset was money – of which she seemed to have plenty. This explained her début with us – from which the Italian management benefited greatly, thank you very much.

She had been cosseted by her vocal teacher until her auspicious début, and had been given only one piece of scenic advice: 'Whatever you do, do it Centre Stage.' To this she adhered religiously.

During one of her first performances, after I, as Leonora, had just 'died' Centre Stage, she took up her last aria and started to move rapidly around my 'corpse' like a headless chicken. Her skirts were swishing and her high heels were clicking only a hair's breadth from my face and hands. Never have I experienced such exquisite agony, knowing that, at any moment, I could be defaced or maimed for life. Her aria ended in a final, wild skirmish, while she came nearer and nearer to me until she landed with her full weight on me – triumphant, and *Centre Stage!*

*

In about 1952 I had also sung Leonora in *La Forza del Destino* with the Dublin opera. The role of Padre Guardiano was sung by Bruce Dargavel, a delightfully laid-back Welsh bass, and in one of the intervals the two of us were chatting about how little rehearsal time singers often have before being thrown on stage. He laughed and told me that he had recently been asked to sing Angelotti in *Tosca* – a part he had not sung before and knew very little about – without any rehearsal or stage directions. I loved the way in which he dolefully said, 'There I was, standin' in the middle of the stage, like a rrruddy bunch o' mint...' – all in his lovely Welsh lilt.

In that production of *La Forza* the cast was all British with the exception of the tenor, an Italian. Having the usual tenorial brain, it had not occurred to him to familiarize himself with the English version we were singing, and, as usual, we had had no rehearsals together. Undaunted, we launched into the First Act, which includes a rather repetitive solo for Leonora. We were still some way from the end of this aria when, without waiting for the conductor's beat, the tenor marched on stage and started singing – a whole page too early for his duet with me. I carried on regardless to the end of my aria and into the duet, as did he – quite an ordeal for both of us.

In the last Act of the opera, as Leonora falls dying, Stage Right (prompt corner), Alvaro rushes on stage from the opposite side, wearing a full-length monk's habit. Unfortunately the stage at Dublin had a dangerously slippery floor, and the tenor's sandals had no grip whatsoever. He slid the whole width of the stage towards my body, his cassock riding up beneath his arms to reveal a pair of sky-blue underpants and scarlet socks. Roars of laughter ... Curtain!

During another performance of *La Forza* I ran up the stairs to my dressing-room, dressed in Leonora's hermit monk's costume and holding my skirts up high. I met a real monk walking down the stairs, his eyes popping and his mouth open in astonishment, clutching his rosary as if he had just encountered the devil.

＊

On my return from the United States in 1948 I had no flat in London, and so I stayed in a small Kensington hotel. I had a radio contract to fulfil in Stockholm soon afterwards, and as I needed to take some cash with me to Sweden, I dropped into my local bank in Shaftesbury Avenue with my passport. As Gene was still in America I was required, for the first time in many years, to organize my own travel arrangements, and I must have been in a rather disorientated state of mind because I left my passport at the bank. I discovered this only when I started to pack that evening.

I had an early flight the next morning for an orchestral rehearsal in the afternoon followed by the broadcast in the evening, and I went cold with panic. Phoning the bank in some wild hope of getting hold of a security officer, there was, of course, no reply. I rang the nearest police station and, explaining my appalling situation, asked their advice. Unbelievably, they offered to ring the bank manager on his home number, which they kept for security reasons. He evidently realized the gravity of the situation, for he phoned me back straight away.

He told me that he lived in Richmond and was willing to go to the Shaftesbury Avenue branch for me, but that he had to have his assistant manager with him as my passport would have been put in the safe, which could be opened only by dual control with the key that each of them possessed. Unfortunately the assistant manager was out at the theatre and was not expected home until eleven-thirty – too late for anything to be done that evening. However, the manager very kindly said that they would be outside the bank at seven-thirty the following morning with my passport. He also explained that he would phone me at five-thirty to make sure that I was awake, and then he wished me goodnight.

At the appointed time next morning I drew up outside the bank in my taxi, much to the bewilderment of the driver, and found two elegantly dressed banking gentlemen holding out my passport for collection. Can anyone imagine this happening today? Furthermore, this was not the end of the story. Arriving with my luggage at the then Cromwell Road Air Terminal (now a Sainsbury's) fifteen minutes before boarding the coach for Heathrow, I realized I had left my luggage keys on my dressing table in the hotel in Kensington.

I frantically phoned the hotel and begged them to send a porter with my keys immediately, if not sooner. Within five minutes I saw the porter hurling himself through the swing doors, slipping on the polished floor, and sliding towards me. He arrived at my feet with his arms and legs sprawling, and threw my keys up at me.

By now it was boarding time, and I had made it. But never again did I go through such panic. I had been taught a very important lesson: think before you leap.

31

Gene's Suicide

IN 1955, when I was at the height of my international operatic career, Iskoldoff started to experience a major financial crisis. As I was obviously worried, a friend recommended a very fine medium to me, and, with nothing to lose, I contacted her. She knew nothing whatsoever about me, and it took her quite some time to find the key to who I was and what I did. Suddenly she said, 'Yes, you are a singer and you have a very large range. You could be a contralto or a coloratura soprano.' She went on to relate various other incidents from my past.

Then she paused, and her face darkened. She said, 'In your last life you were a ballet dancer who committed suicide at the age of forty. And I see very clearly that a disaster is facing you which will wreck your life. When you reach that same age, which is not far away, you will again wish to commit suicide. I beg you not to do it. If you do, you will pay dearly for it and will have to return, once again, to redeem yourself.'

Iskoldoff's last enterprise in England was the Italian Opera Company at the Stoll, followed by several tours of the UK. He never seemed to see the dangers that were obvious even to me. He thought he knew it all, and would never take any advice. I was told to stick to my singing and to leave the business side of things to him.

Our final tour was in 1956. The Suez crisis, with its resulting shortage of petrol, and the sudden boom in TV viewing combined to create huge problems for many theatrical enterprises, especially in the provinces. We suffered excruciatingly, particularly as the Italians saw Iskoldoff's vulnerable position and started to cheat him even more aggressively. The losses started coming in. And rather than declaring himself officially bankrupt, Iskoldoff, in the middle of a nervous breakdown, committed suicide.

At the time of his death, Iskoldoff and I were still very close friends, and I had seen the disaster coming. I tried to warn his wife, with whom he had been reunited at the time of my marriage to Igor Semiletoff, but her response was to call me a manic-depressive and to tell me to pull myself together. In order to help him financially as much as I could, I had taken no salary at all for the last months of the Italian Opera, and had also pawned every-thing of value that I had. Of course, I lost it all in the end, and was left literally without the proverbial dime. A suicide often has an unpleasant aftermath – tactful silences or embarrassed twitterings – and only one friend suggested lending me some cash, on the condition that it was used for the purpose of arranging my three-roomed flat so that one or two rooms could be let to help me financially.

Destitute, isolated, and desperately alone, I was indeed very close to suicide myself. But I never considered it as a final solution, however grave the problems. I have always had the feeling that a person who commits suicide is then forced to cool his or her heels in some awful limbo, awaiting their allotted end. So I did not kill myself, but instead of physical suicide I committed vocal, moral, suicide. Singing had been my lifeblood, and I chose to die a vocal death.

*

During the life of the Italian Opera Company in London and on tour, the singers and members of the orchestra were divided into two entities, as if they had nothing in common. Most of the musi-cians were therefore complete strangers to me, and we remained thus even on train journeys. But there was just one player with whom there seemed to be some vague contact, and if we met in the street he would at least say hello. One day this musician (alas, I cannot remember his name, and wish I could) rang me to say how deeply sorry he was to hear about Gene's death, and then, apologiz-ing in advance for his next question, asked me how my finances were.

Amazed by this unexpected sympathy, I told him in fairly broken tones that I was penniless. He said he had suspected this, and promised to contact the Musicians' Benevolent Fund in the hope that they might help me. This was the first I had ever heard of the organization. A few days later he rang again and asked if he could visit me as he had something for me. When he arrived, I realized that what I had suspected was true: he was obviously a very heavy drinker. His appearance was sad, to say the least – dishevelled and uncared for.

He handed me an envelope containing forty pounds from the Musicians' Benevolent Fund. I was astounded by this kindness, which overwhelmed me. I would never have dreamed of contacting the Fund myself, and so I thanked him and we had a chat. He was an Australian – in his forties, I would think – and he seemed sad and lonely. I invited him for dinner the following week, thinking that this would be a small way in which I could return his thoughtful kindness and that it might also cheer him up and give him something to look forward to.

The day of the dinner date came. I had prepared a pleasant three-course meal, and waited for the doorbell to ring. I waited and waited, but still no one came. Finally, at about ten o'clock in the evening, I rang his digs – he was living in what sounded like a very dreary bedsitter – and asked to speak to him. The sad voice on the other end of the phone told me that his body had just been discovered in his room – he had taken his own life. My grief and sense of guilt were almost unbearable. If only I had known. If only he had come to dinner. Perhaps both our lives would have been different.

✳

My efforts, albeit short-lived, to find a new agent or manager all led to the same request: cash or 'personal favours'. As I did not have the former, and did not wish to part with the latter, I had no choice but to give up my career. I retired gracefully to became a secretary (thank God for my shorthand of so many decades earlier) and 'came up for air' whenever the occasional singing engagement came along. These were offshoots of my earlier career, and included *Eugene Onegin* in Scandinavia and several important BBC concerts including the Proms.

I would be given a contract six weeks before the performance, and would use that short period to learn whatever I had to learn and to get my voice back to near-perfection. No one suspected a thing! However, these engagements often involved weeks of rehearsal as well as studying a new part, and for this I had no financial wherewithal whatsoever. As I could not afford to give up my secretarial work during these periods, I was forced to practise and rehearse with my pianist, Colin Tilney, in the evenings.

I suppose that every time I received an offer to sing, I secretly hoped it would lead to something continuous and consistent. But it never did, and so, little by little, I accepted the inevitable. My final broadcast for the BBC was in 1965, when I was still on the top of my form. In fact, I had reached an interpretative maturity that even I find fascinating. But it seems that it all fell on deaf ears. Not having an agent to push me was doubtless part of the reason, but then I had never needed one for the BBC: they always came to me direct! However, no one at the 'Beeb' ever seemed able to fulfil promises of future engagements, and by the time I contacted them as requested, they had moved to a totally different department and were no longer able to carry out the projects we had discussed. They seemed to be a people forever on the move.

＊

In 1997 a friend of a friend met a representative of the Musicians' Benevolent Fund and my name was mentioned in their conversation, although the context is not known to me. The representative tentatively asked about my financial situation, and was disturbed to hear that it was in fact pretty disastrous. A couple of days later I received a wonderful letter from the representative, suggesting that she came to see me to discuss my situation with a view to assisting me in whatever way was possible.

To my enormous relief, the Fund found a way to help me overcome a lot of the financial problems that were destroying my life. The Fund does its work in a most tactful manner, making you feel as if *it* is grateful for *your* acceptance, and I can honestly say that for the first time in my life I had a sense of financial security. The point of the story, however, is this: the representative came to see me recently on one of her regular check-up visits, and said, 'You know, we help an awful lot of young artists if things go wrong with their careers.' I replied that I had always been under the impression that the Fund assisted only retired musicians or their beneficiaries, and told her the story about the Australian musician and the envelope of money. I then asked if I could have benefited from a more substantial amount than the forty pounds. 'Of course', she replied. 'We could have helped you a lot.'

I explained that there had been no follow-up at all, and was told that in those rather early days of the Fund's existence it was assumed that if the artist in question did not make further contact with the organization, then he or she was OK. Now, it has developed a far wider-reaching efficiency and it checks up on each case to ensure that the artist is not too embarrassed to make further requests for help. Remembering the envelope given to me by the Australian forty years earlier, and realizing how much further I could have been helped by the Fund to continue my career, I then made myself block out from my mind the full meaning of what I had just learned.

＊

Writing of the Musicians' Benevolent Fund reminds me of another of the many occasions in my life when coincidence has come into play. When I was sixteen I worked for a short time as an apprentice in a very swish London boutique by the name of Peter Studio, situated in a row of shops at the Regents Park end of Baker Street.

The manageress was a Miss Elwes, a name I have always remembered in connection with what I recognized in her as a member of the upper crust – the first such person I had ever encountered. Her manner intrigued me with its typically casual, offhand way characteristic of the upper echelons, and although I studied her with both a sense of awe and also a strong awareness of myself as an outsider, I found her extremely pleasant. The name Elwes often appeared in gossip columns and society reviews, and it always caught my attention and continued to fascinate me.

More than sixty years later a neighbour rang me to say that a young friend of hers, a portraitist by the name of Gervase Elwes, had heard my *Desert Island Discs* broadcast and was keen to meet me with a view to painting a miniature of me. This was his speciality (he usually painted famous people in the costumes of a comic figure or character) and I could hardly believe my ears. We met, and he did indeed paint a miniature of me; so another link was made with the past of so many years earlier. He, of course, is a great-nephew of the famous tenor Gervase Elwes, in whose memory the Musicians' Benevolent Fund was founded.

A few months ago I went to an exhibition of wonderful caricatures of the famous by the young Gervase. The gallery was full of many other Elweses – cousins, second cousins, nieces, nephews, and so on. I spoke to several of them, who seemed to know very little about their far-reaching family, and I was both amazed and amused that not one of them had ever heard of their brilliant tenorial forebear – not so long departed ... The poignancy of his appallingly unnecessary death still brings a shiver to the spine: he was in Boston, seeing a friend off at a railway station, and was carrying a coat belonging to the friend over his arm. As the train pulled out, Gervase remembered the coat and tried to pass it to his friend; the coat caught in the train door and dragged Gervase to his death. I once heard someone remark that he was giving as he was dying, and so it is appropriate that the Musicians' Benevolent Fund exists in his memory.

I would like to add that I have been helped enormously not only by the Musicians' Benevolent Fund but also by that wonderful charitable organization, the Royal United Kingdom Beneficent Association (RUKBA). Thanks to a friend who, unbeknown to me, put my case before them, they approached me with an offer of assistance for which I am deeply grateful.

32

Deréta Skirts

As I WAS DESTITUTE when Gene died, it was imperative that I find work – of any kind. Glancing through the *Evening Standard*, I saw an advertisement that read: LADY REQUIRED TO COOK DIRECTORS' LUNCHEONS FOR DERÉTA SKIRT COMPANY. Some madness in me prompted me to ring for an appointment – I suppose I was literally testing the water.

The following day, looking as inconspicuous as I could, I knocked on the Deréta Skirts office door, and was confronted by an attractive woman in her early twenties, sitting at a desk. She gave me a very odd look and handed me a form to complete. This stymied me for a moment, as I had never anticipated having to fill in paperwork when applying for a job. I quickly decided to use an abbreviated version of my married name – Kyra Semile – but was forced to leave most of the form empty. After all, what experience, and what credentials, did I have to be a professional cook?

Having hesitatingly returned the form to the young lady, I watched her glance at it and then at me – very directly. 'Is this your real name?', she asked. When I told her that it was, she replied, 'I know another Kyra. Her surname is Vayne.' The look on my face was enough to confirm her suspicions, and I rose to leave. She said, 'Miss Vayne, I have stood for hours in the rain and the snow to hear your Tosca. For me, you are the greatest. What on earth has happened to you?' By now she was weeping, and I myself was on the verge of tears.

I implored her not to enquire as to what had happened, explaining simply that I had experienced a great personal tragedy and that I had to work – doing anything, if necessary. Sobbing, she replied that it was a question of her or me; she could not bring herself to take my application form to the directors, and in any case, she would have to leave Deréta Skirts if I were given the job, as there was no way that she could work alongside me. I understood completely, and begged her not to give the matter another thought. I made my way out of the office, leaving her still crying bitterly.

✳

In 1995 I gave a talk at Farringdons Records in London, and was mobbed by many supporters, from both the 'old' life and the 'new'.

While I was signing my CDs I became aware of a very elegant middle-aged lady patiently waiting to speak to me. When I came up for air she said to me, 'You were the greatest Tosca I have ever seen.' I laughed, and thanked her. Then she continued, 'Do you remember coming to Deréta Skirts one day?' Puzzled, I thought for a moment and replied, 'Not offhand. But I may have done so. Did I buy something lovely?'

'You hadn't come to buy, Miss Vayne', she replied. 'You came for a job interview.' Suddenly I remembered that poignant afternoon thirty-eight years earlier, and recognized in this lady the young girl who had been so distressed by my situation. By this time she was embracing me and sobbing quietly; I, too, was in tears, but I could see that she was pleased by what had eventually happened to me. Further words seemed superfluous, but before we nodded goodbye and her figure disappeared, I managed to say, 'My phone number is in the directory. Do please ring me; I'd love to talk with you.'

I was deeply moved by her courage in confronting me with something so traumatic and private between the two of us. She never contacted me again – perhaps she thought it would be too painful for both of us to dwell on what had happened – but I still hope that she might.

33

Vsevolod Petrie, Aka 'Seva'

ONE OF THE ODDEST THINGS about my life is that although I knew only a very few Russian people after reaching adulthood, practically all my personal relationships have been with Russians and all of them have been disastrous. It seems that some of us never learn from our mistakes.

As I have already explained, the trauma of Gene's death and its appalling aftermath left me desperately isolated. Failure (for that is how my situation was perceived in most people's minds) brings with it little sympathy; and, having no family or anyone really close, I received none. Jealousy, both professional and social, plays a very large part in a career, and often, instead of sympathy, one gets almost a sense of rejoicing from one's friends, or at least from those one thought were one's friends.

Soon after Gene's suicide, an old acquaintance suggested that I sing in the Russian church in Ennismore Gardens. This seemed a good idea, since my voice could at least be utilized without any great effort. So one Sunday I went to the church to listen to the choir and to see if I could perhaps assist it in some way. Then I contacted the choirmaster and offered my services. At the very first rehearsal it seemed, once again, as if I were causing a stir, both good and bad. As before, I felt the familiar wave of suspicion and resentment from the female members of the choir, and once again I was a danger to the security of others.

I also became aware that one of the younger men in the choir seemed fascinated by me and could hardly take his eyes off me. Later he told me he had noticed me in the congregation on the first day that I came to the church. He fell in love with my back view, so to speak. He accompanied me home after every rehearsal, and although I did not accept him seriously, I at least felt less alone than before.

Vsevolod Petrie, known as Seva, was of Russian origin, born in Brest-Litovsk on the Russian/Polish border, and his parents were both dead. During the war he joined the Polish forces and had a tremendously tough innings in Italy and elsewhere. It was a miracle that he came out of the conflict alive. He had studied civil engineering and had found a very good position with Ove-Arup, a large international firm that ultimately won the contract to build the Sydney Opera House.

After a few weeks it was obvious that he was far from well, and the next thing I heard was that he was in hospital. The news was very frightening: he had cancer of the colon, and the situation was literally touch and go. I knew him far too little to be involved in all this, and did not visit him. Some time later he reappeared at re-hearsals looking decidedly fragile. He told me that, after his opera-tion, a priest had been called to give him the Last Rites; in his semi-conscious state he had seen my image before him, and this had saved him, giving him the strength to fight and come through. By now we had grown closer, and soon our relationship ripened into what seemed to be a mutual love.

I was then working as a secretary for the British Standards Institution, and it seemed logical for Seva to come and live in my Queen's Gate flat. His health was not one hundred per cent and he seemed haunted by some natural fear. After his first check-up fol-lowing the operation, his surgeon asked to speak to me privately and told me, in no uncertain manner, that Seva was seriously ill and had about six months to live. He suggested that I should do my best to make his final months as comfortable as possible, and told me to pull myself together, stop my tears, repair my make-up, and go out full of optimism to face Seva. This I did, in no way showing my internal grief.

For a while it seemed as if this strategy were working; but then, unfortunately, a 'kind' friend told Seva the truth about his 'death sentence'. It was hard for us to live with this knowledge, and I decided to look for help from the very famous faith healer Harry Edwards, who had worked miracles many times. After much per-suasion, I took Seva to his clinic. Knowing nothing about Seva, or what was wrong with him, Edwards' reaction was astonishing. His hand went straight to the spot where the operation had been car-ried out and he held it there for quite a long period, concentrating his mind in an almost hypnotic manner. He then spoke a few confident words, full of hope, and from that moment onwards Seva started to recover. His progress was slow but continuous.

Seva, however, was not an easy person to live with. He showed no interest whatsoever in my now almost dormant singing career, nor did he try to help me with my new life. On the occasions when I returned to sing either at the Royal Festival Hall or the Royal Albert Hall, or for the BBC, he seemed unable to relate to this aspect of my life and became resentful. For instance, I was invited by the BBC to sing Stravinsky's *Les Noces* with Janet Baker and John Mitchison at the Royal Festival Hall, with Bruno Maderna conducting. I vaguely thought, or rather hoped, that Seva would take me out to dinner after the concert; but not being sure, I had gone out and bought provisions in case it was necessary to make sandwiches.

When we arrived home after the concert I was still on a slight high because of the personal success I had enjoyed and the thrill of once again singing in public. However, Seva behaved with total disregard for me. I sat down, still in my lovely evening dress and make-up, and asked him, 'Would you be an angel, Seva, and make some sandwiches? Everything is laid out in the kitchen.' With a look of insolent amazement, he replied, 'And what's wrong with *you* doing it?' That night I went to bed feeling very hungry and deeply unhappy.

Seva had no hobbies. He did not read, and the theatre was of no interest whatsoever to him. He was also tremendously indolent when at home, taking no part in anything domestic or social. Even shopping was beneath him. I perhaps mistakenly put all this down to his traumatic experiences in the war and his recent illness, and did my utmost to give him a comfortable home with every possible amenity. For his sake I even went so far as to consult a psychiatrist, which cost me a lot of money that I did not then have. I told the psychiatrist our story and explained that our relationship was seriously deteriorating; the reply was that I was to forget myself and my ex-career, and to think only of Seva, who mattered far more than I. It was then that I finally decided to allow what was left of my career to phase out, and to do nothing more to further it by seeking engagements. I stuck to this decision, and devoted my entire time to Seva.

Yet he never lifted a finger to help me in any way. Everything I did in the home was taken for granted, even after I had worked long hours at the office. In his opinion, that was what a woman was there for. Although, in terms of his health, he never looked back, our relationship started going downhill even more rapidly. Weekends, for which I longed, became a nightmare. Seva would go off, just as I was ready with Saturday lunch, to watch football with his buddy, after which they would drink themselves senseless. He would eventually drive home at around two or three in the morning, fall into bed, and remain there until late on the Sunday afternoon.

Once again I had allowed myself to become trapped. But my one aim was to wait for his 'all clear' to be confirmed, and I thought no further ahead than that. During this period we were also often apart. I was offered an opera season in Denmark, he went to Plymouth to work on the new town centre (this was at the end of the 1950s), and I then went off to the States for six months. The moment his all clear came through, I knew the time had come for us to call it a day.

This happened suddenly and very peacefully in 1963. Arriving, stoned, after another of his binges, Seva fiddled with the front door key, fell in through the door, and crawled into the bedroom on all fours. I very quietly said that I had made up a bed for him in the sitting-room as I no longer wished to lose sleep from his snoring and his alcoholic fumes. He gingerly got up off the floor and, slurring his words, muttered that he would either sleep in the bedroom, or leave. I replied that the decision was his and that he had just made it: all he had to do was to pick up his toothbrush and anything else essential and to shut the door behind him. This is what he did. A few weeks later he made a couple of attempts to patch things up, but to no avail.

✳

In 1995, after reading an article about me in the *Daily Telegraph*, Seva rang up an old ex-mutual friend and suggested that she write to me asking for tickets for the talk, publicized in the article, that I was going to give at Farringdons Records. I received her letter with some shock, and decided to ignore it.

On the night of my talk the audience were having drinks and chatting upstairs while I was giving various radio and media interviews downstairs. A few minutes before I was to begin the talk I went upstairs to have a drink, and, sitting down, I suddenly felt a figure loom up before me. Without looking, I instinctively knew it was Seva. He asked, 'Don't you recognize me?' Still not looking at him, I replied, 'I do not *wish* to recognize you.' When he questioned this, and asked the reason, I told him, 'Because I don't recall a moment's happiness with you. You are the last person I want to see.'

All this happened in one of those strange moments of complete silence where every word rings clear, for all to hear. Then, to rid myself of a tremendous burst of rage, I turned to the person on my right and said in a resounding voice, 'That's the bastard who finally finished me off!' It was certainly a field day for the media, for it was they who were sitting next to me.

34

Father

A s MY FATHER may appear to readers a rather shadowy figure in the background of my life, I feel he deserves a clearer portrayal than the nebulous one I have so far drawn. Furthermore, I have discovered that many once-buried memories of him now demand recognition, thereby inevitably taking on a new and different meaning. One of them was, perhaps, too terrifying to acknowledge at the time.

Father had a lifelong habit of taking a late-night, boiling hot bath and then dozing in it until the wee hours. One night in 1929, he went off to his ablutions as usual, but at about midnight, my mother and I awoke to a strong smell of gas coming from under the kitchen door – as was often the case in those days, our large kitchen also contained a board-camouflaged bath. We tried to open the door but found it to be locked. We yelled, we screamed, but to no avail. As the stench of gas was becoming ever stronger, I phoned the police in a panic. They quickly arrived, smashed open the kitchen door, and found Father unconscious, lying face down with his head inside the oven door in a pool of blood. The gas tap was fully open.

When the tightly locked windows were opened, the room soon cleared of the fumes, and Father came to. Sizing up his situation, he started vehemently proclaiming that the heat of the bath water had knocked him senseless and that, as he fell, his head had hit the oven door – hence the blood. He also claimed that his hand had been raised protectively as he fell, and that this is what had snapped open the gas tap. It all sounded fairly plausible to me, and I accepted his explanation without questioning it. But as I escorted the police downstairs and out of the building, one of the officers remarked to me, 'This was most certainly a potential suicide' – a rather tactless thing to say to a girl of thirteen about her father, and one that I did not believe. Father would *not* have committed suicide, I was sure.

Trying to lessen Father's obvious embarrassment, Mother and I went straight back to bed. And as far as I can recall, the incident was never discussed again – certainly not in front of me. In time, it became hazily unimportant and I forgot about it – until recently, when it rolled before me like an old film. Suddenly the significance of that year, 1929, hit me like a thunderbolt: following the American stock market crash, Father had lost his job at Brandt's Bank; and once again, poor man, his life was in ruins. Yet I still have one nagging doubt about what happened that night. Why the *falling* into the oven? Why the blood? *Was* it an accident, or ... ? I shall never know.

✳

When Father lost his job at the bank he had difficulty finding any employment. But the word 'cannot' was not in his vocabulary, and whatever work came his way, he did it well. After a succession of odd accounting jobs, he joined John Stafford Productions, a film company, and worked there for several years until the beginning of the war, when the company closed down. Once again, he was out of work and desperate.

Although now in his sixties, he volunteered as a crewmember on one of the 'little boats' that scurried to and fro between Dover and Dunkirk until that heroic rescue operation was finally complete. Then, by a fluke, he became an engine inspector for Sercks Radiators, based in London and Birmingham and owned by an old friend of his from Russia. After the war he moved to Birmingham, and was doing remarkable inspection work for Sercks right up to his death at the age of eighty-three.

✳

I remember that when my bizarre marriage ended in disaster, Father told me bitterly, 'One should *never* return to one's first love.' At the time, I interpreted his remark as cynicism, but I later realized that in marrying Igor I had in fact emulated Father in his gallantry towards my mother. I, too, had gone to the aid of my first love, and what a price I paid. Was it smaller or greater than Father's? One thing is certain: had Father not done what he did, I would not be writing these words now.

Throughout his life, our relationship was either on or off. To outsiders, he appeared enormously proud of my success, but he was incapable of showing this to me – as if unable to reconcile the figure of the opera singer with his own daughter. He wanted the kudos for himself, and did not wish in any way to share it with me by acknowledging my success. I eventually worked out that he could not accept my achievements because this would merely underline his own lack of success. He was in fact a brilliant man, who in no sense could be considered a failure. But although there was nothing that he could not do, he never did anything remarkable.

The fact that I was a woman, as well as successful, only made matters worse for him.

At times, too, he even appeared not to relate to me on a personal level. For example, as I was preparing to return home after one of my visits to him in Birmingham, I told him that I would come and see him again soon; his reply was, 'Is there any point? We don't really have anything in common.'

*

By 1959 I had largely given up my singing career, but that year I went on one of my occasional broadcasting visits to Stockholm. After singing there, I flew on to Finland for another broadcast, conducted by the young Paavo Berglund. He was then making his name in his own country before coming to England, where for many years he conducted the Bournemouth Symphony and several other orchestras.

On the plane I sat next to a charming businessman who, after we had chatted for a while, invited me for lunch the following day. He picked me up at my hotel and took me to a swish restaurant right on the harbour, pointing out a very elegant club attached to it. I suddenly had an amazing sense of *déjà vu*, realizing that *this* was the sports club to which Father had belonged in his youth – long, long ago. He had shown me photographs of it and talked of it with affection; and the experience of actually seeing the building before my eyes was very strange indeed. While in Finland I also had the pleasure of contacting a close friend of my father's from the early days, with whom I was able to gossip at length.

My relationship with Father was quite amicable during this period, and as I sat on the plane during the journey back to England, my mind was full of the exciting things I had seen and heard in Finland, things that I could share with him. But it was well after nine p.m. when I arrived home and, remembering that he hated late evening phone calls, I decided not to ring him until the following day. At about ten p.m. the phone rang, and I heard the voice of Father's landlady in Birmingham tell me in broken tones that he was ill. She promised to phone later with more news; and at eleven-thirty she phoned to say that he had died – he had in fact already gone when she made the first phone call, but she had not felt able to break the news to me in one fell swoop.

So Father was gone, and I was left alone. There was no way that I could sleep that night, and I made no attempt to. I sat and meditated deeply, and in that no-man's-land of thought, I felt his presence with me. Somehow we conversed – wordlessly, and at length. We forgave each other what there was to forgive, and were at peace with each other as never before. We had reached an understanding. Above all, he was now no longer crippled by his fear of weakness.

Just as my mother left her mark on me – her hospitality, and her philosophies of '*Qui excuse s'accuse*' and 'Never let the sun go down upon your wrath' – so Father marked me indelibly. Independence at all costs, never asking for favours ... and, of course, there is no such word as 'cannot'. Yet I feel strongly that without such firm convictions, my life would actually have been an easier one, and my career more opportune. Thank God that I have no progeny through which to continue these damaging beliefs!

35

The Players Theatre Club

F OUR YEARS AGO, following the release of my first CD, I started to give a number of 'reminiscence talks', and Yogi, the owner of the general store opposite my flat, showed great enthusiasm about my sudden burst of fame. Without saying a word to me, he stuck a small flyer for one of my talks in his shop window. Several local people who knew me extremely well by sight suddenly put a name to my face, and among them was someone whom I knew as Tony Bateman – an ex-theatre pro with whom I had often chatted about this and that.

On my next visit to the shop, Yogi said, 'This is for you!' and handed me a large buff envelope that Tony had triumphantly given him to pass on to me. On opening it, I was staggered to find a whole batch of publicity material relating to a long engagement I had had with the famous Players Theatre Club when they went to New York under the American name of The Strollers. This episode of my career was one that I had put to the back of my mind and rarely thought about. It transpired that Tony had also been in the company, but, unbelievably, we had not recognized each other. He is a gentle, retiring person who was not given to throwing his weight around, as did the other members of the company – which is why I had, in a way, 'passed him over'. In order to complete the picture of how and why I joined this rather cult-like theatrical group, it is necessary to go back thirty-four years.

One day in 1961, as I was on my way to a job as a secretarial temp, I bumped into Olga Stringfellow, an old Australian friend from my singing days. She was delighted to see me again, and immediately put forward an amazing suggestion: would I like a trip to New York? She had recently met a member of the famous and wealthy Woolworth family who was sponsoring an American entrepreneur by the name of John Krimsky in his venture of taking the Players Theatre to New York as a dinner entertainment in a swish venue (formerly the famous El Morocco Club) on East 54th Street. They were wildly searching for a first-class singer to perform operatic arias and Edwardian ballads, dressed in the appropriate costumes. (The famous Players had started life as a late evening cabaret theatre of the Edwardian era, a superb evocation of 'Olde

Time' Variety. Its venue in Villiers Street, just off the Strand and underneath Charing Cross arches, was enormously popular for many years.)

It so happened that, during this particular week, I was fulfilling one of my surprise engagements from the BBC – singing Stravinsky's *Les Noces* at the Proms under the baton of Andrew (now Sir Andrew) Davis. This was a great showcase for my talent, and I could not have wished for a better venue with which to impress the Americans. It clinched a contract with them, and they booked me there and then.

At this point I must underline the fact that these important engagements by the BBC came to me out of the blue, each time giving me the wild hope that my career could burgeon once again. In fact I sang *Les Noces* three times for the BBC, in consecutive years: firstly in a concert at the Royal Festival Hall under the baton of Bruno Maderna; and twice at the Proms, the second time conducted by Sir John Pritchard. (At this performance, Shostakovich was in the audience and came backstage afterwards to congratulate the artists. Sir John said, 'Thank *God* there's someone here who speaks Russian, who can talk to him in his own language', and asked me to act as an interpreter for the great composer's conversations with the assembled performers.) But alas, these and my other BBC engagements were all one-offs, and my career never regained the momentum it once had.

Before leaving for New York, I had an initial trial run with the Players Theatre in London. Unfortunately they were an extremely tightly knit coterie – very 'lovey-dovey' – and I, being an intruder in their midst, felt the draught very painfully. They were unwilling to include me, defeating all my efforts to merge and be friends with them. But I was almost delirious at what seemed like another godsend to my career, and I was determined to use this opportunity, this last big chance, to find my way onto the American musical scene. My voice was still at its peak, and I decided that once I had crossed the Atlantic I would audition for *everyone*.

I remember that when I arrived in New York I was bowled over by life-sized posters of Joan Sutherland stuck on every possible surface – she was about to make her début in the city. But this was not going to deter me in the least. (In a way, I had caught up with her again, for while I was living in the flat in Queen's Gate she and her husband, Richard Bonynge, bought a house in nearby Gloucester Road. After that, I often used to see her in the local shops – at first on her own, and later pushing a pram!)

Meanwhile, a great friend of mine in London, the actor Derek Aylward, had passed my details to the famous (perhaps one might now say infamous) Ed Smith, the greatest recording 'pirate' of our day, who made a bomb by selling great performances recorded live all over the world with equipment concealed on his person. No sooner had The Strollers opened in New York, to great success, than I started to receive letters from Ed Smith. 'Do nothing', he wrote. 'Sing for no one until I contact you. I have something really big for you.' Knowing his fame as a fixer, I did what he suggested, and waited. Another note came from him, containing a similar message, and so I continued to wait, not daring to spoil what could be a golden opportunity. In time, a third note arrived, explaining that he and Martinelli were organizing a company of singers to appear on television in a vast repertoire of operas. I would be given all the roles suitable to so versatile an artist as I.

I continued to wait, with bated breath, and soon afterwards met Ed Smith. He was full of promises, and took me to Martinelli, the artistic director of the new venture, so that he could hear me sing. I sang; Martinelli listened in ecstasy. 'A God-given voice', he raved, and we shook hands. It was in the bag. And then ... silence. And more silence. And that was that. Ed had taken on more than he could chew, and was busy extricating himself from some tight corners – his recording ploys were becoming too obvious, and he was on the brink of big trouble.

While waiting for developments, I did go to meet a very powerful agent in New York, but he told me that without winning a big vocal competition in the USA I stood no chance whatsoever. I spent about six months in New York with The Strollers, but the rest, as the saying goes, is history; once again, personal problems intruded on, and destroyed, my professional life – or rather, I stupidly allowed them to. As I will explain shortly, another miraculous opportunity was wasted by my insane sense of responsibility towards someone close to me who was demanding help. Once more, I was defeated.

36

Zara Dolukhanova

WHEN I WENT to a recital given by the Russian mezzo Zara Dolukhanova at the Royal Festival Hall in 1966, I was struck by her unassuming manner, her elegance, and, of course, her voice. She was different in every way from the normal Soviet artists I had heard; these other women were always brassy, with shrill voices and a rather vulgar platform manner. In contrast, I felt a real empathy with Dolukhanova. Her voice was rich and technically perfect, her interpretation deep and considered. In fact I was sufficiently smitten to do something that I have very seldom done: I went backstage to congratulate her and to make a contact.

We seemed to have an instant rapport, and chatted pleasantly. She then requested a small favour from me. I was delighted to be asked, and enquired what she wanted. She told me that in a couple of days' time she would be giving a recital in a shop in Oxford Street and, not knowing quite what this would involve, she felt nervous at the prospect. I immediately realized that the shop was John Lewis, which had a beautiful concert hall where I had heard some wonderful recitals and performances of chamber operas. I explained how delightful the venue was and that she would enjoy performing there. She then told me that she was going to be presented to one of the shop's directors and asked if I would act as her interpreter.

The recital was a great success, and it gave me enormous pleasure to interpret for her. Before leaving the concert, I invited her to visit me at home and she accepted with delight. She warned, however, that the arrangements would have to be made with her accompanist, who would love to come too. The accompanist in question was quite obviously her KGB minder, an over-made-up and heavily peroxided blonde, typically brash and over-confident. I addressed her, inviting her to join Dolukhanova on her visit to me and giving her my telephone number, which she jotted down on a sheet of music.

Dolukhanova rang the next day to thank me for my help and to beg me not to go to too much trouble in entertaining them both. She also asked me to be so kind as to pick them up from their hotel in Kensington as, not speaking English and not knowing London, they could easily lose their way. She had obviously chosen a moment of freedom from her minder in which to talk to me, and we chatted for quite a time. However, most of her remarks were slightly ambiguous, as if she were trying to tell me something by inference rather than directly in words. Our conversation ended rather abruptly, and I arranged to be there at four-thirty the following afternoon.

I had invited two very close friends of mine to my little party. One was Colin Tilney, my former accompanist, who had composed a piece of music specially for Dolukhanova, and the other was Richard Samuel from the Foreign Office. Both spoke Russian superbly. I arrived at the hotel as arranged, and asked the receptionist to phone Dolukhanova and tell her I was waiting for her. I was told that she and the minder were out, and that the staff had no idea when they would be returning. After waiting for half an hour I asked for some paper and wrote a rather perfunctory note explaining how long I had been at the hotel and that I could wait no longer. Then I returned home, where Colin and Richard were holding the fort in my absence.

Richard embraced me and said that although he had not wanted to disillusion me in case he was wrong, he had recognized the scenario. However much Dolukhanova longed to visit me, there was no way the powers-that-be would allow her to. He added that within a few minutes the phone would ring and that Dolukhanova would apologize profusely for being so late. Shortly afterwards the phone did indeed ring, and I asked Richard to answer it. Sure enough, the apologies came fast and furious: she and the accompanist had been held up in a traffic jam.

I felt shattered – more for Dolukhanova than for myself. She was a prisoner who was given freedom to perform before being taken back to the 'cell'. Although she received tremendous acclaim on both occasions that she came to London, this was to be her last visit. I always felt that my contacting her put paid to any further singing engagements here – or in Europe, for that matter. However, only the other day a friend rang from Moscow and said, among other things, 'Dolukhanova sends you her love.' And so yet another little circle in my life has been rounded off. I wonder what she thought of me back in 1966, and what she would make of me now . . .

37

Maya

I FIND IT EXTREMELY DIFFICULT to write about my sister Maya, and I wish I did not have to do so. But as she played such an important and incisive part in the ups and downs of my life, I have no choice. I make no indictment of her, and no accusations towards her; but I am left with a sense of deep disappointment at the lack of encouragement or support that I received from so close a member of my family – someone, indeed, for whom I was prepared to give myself unreservedly and without question.

Either through the circumstances surrounding her early childhood, or simply due to her individual character, Maya was an extremely domineering and aggressive person. There was a latent violence in her that was never far from the surface, and for as far back as I can remember, she had some odd power over me – physically and mentally. Whenever I have thought about her, I have been conscious of my vulnerability towards her and what later became my fear of her – a great fear, in fact, that sometimes left no room for reasoning and which I therefore cannot quite explain.

As a child, Maya was extremely pretty, and was spoilt and cosseted. When I was born she ceased to be the centre of attention, and became markedly jealous of me. I think this often happens – the sudden fall from favour must be a very cruel shock – and quite possibly the parents are more to blame than the child in question.

During our waiting period in Moscow before we rejoined Father in Petrograd, we lived in appalling conditions with no pattern to life whatsoever. As I mentioned earlier, Maya had no option but to join the 'unlooked-after' – dangerously delinquent youngsters who ran around in gangs, pilfering, rifling, and stealing, with no one in authority to stop them. It was simply a question of the survival of the fittest. So, little by little, Maya learned aggression, assertiveness, and a conviction that she alone was right while everyone else was wrong. In time, this pattern of behaviour became a way of life for her.

On our arrival in London in 1924 Maya and I both joined a school where I was frequently victimized for my timidity and lack of English. Unfortunately Maya never came to my rescue; in fact, she joined the 'baddies'. Her extreme bossiness took on quite an ugly turn, and there was no way that I could stand up for myself. At times I was panic-stricken by the way I was treated.

In 1928 Father sent Maya to a high-faluting finishing school in Brussels for a year. Alas, due to the Stock Market crash in 1929, I was not able to follow suit. But it often happens that, just as very pretty children grow up to be far plainer-looking than anticipated, so plain-looking children become much more attractive in later years. Such was the case with us. Maya lost her looks and became rather ordinary in appearance. She seemed to have little taste, particularly in clothing, and she never looked remotely elegant or *soignée*. In contrast, I grew into what I now realize was an attractive woman, developed a flair for clothes, and became one of those fortunate people who can wear the proverbial sack and still look well dressed. This incensed Maya and added to her jealousy of me, particularly in view of my recently-discovered singing voice.

I began my career on the bottom rung, and worked my way up without any encouragement from either Father or Maya. So when my beloved mother died, I was really on my own. Maya was by now a nurse, but seemed ashamed of this fact, threatening me if I ever divulged her profession to any friends that I had. She resented my voice, and I remember her telling someone that *she* had the voice and that I merely sang. When I left home in 1943 our relations deteriorated still further, and there were long periods of silence between us.

At the end of the war Maya began work in Germany for the United Nations Relief and Rehabilitation Administration, an organization dealing with the repatriation of war prisoners. Around 1949 she returned to England but was then homeless because she had rented out the family flat. She inferred that I should help her. At that time, I was living with Eugene Iskoldoff in Westbourne Grove, and knowing Maya's manipulative nature, her jealousy of me, and her harrassing manner, I realized that I could in no way invite her to stay with us. However, Gene became stroppy and revealed that he had very strong family feelings – perhaps through having no family of his own. Nothing that I said made any difference, and he insisted that I invite Maya to stay. As always, I gave in.

To my amazement, she accepted my invitation as if she were doing me a great favour – on condition that, for a salary, she would be our housekeeper. In other words, she would not accept my hospitality, but would agree to be employed by me. I was appalled. My instinct had unfortunately been correct, and in fact the outcome of her sojourn with us was an even greater nightmare than I could have anticipated.

I was mostly on tour during this period, doing Variety with Vic Oliver during the week and returning on Saturday nights ready for a hectic Sunday of broadcasts of *Vic Oliver Introduces* ... followed by a concert with his British Symphony Orchestra. Then on the Monday I would travel to the next town on our current tour. Although I gave Maya quite a hefty housekeeping allowance, there was very little to show for it. When, one Monday morning, I said that I would like an early lunch prior to my journey, she simply replied, 'I don't eat lunch.' And that was that. It got to the point where I almost dreaded coming home, and for obvious reasons, Gene went out for meals more and more frequently.

As I have already explained, when I had an important concert at the Royal Albert Hall with Boris Christoff my rehearsals with the orchestra were virtually non-existent. As a result, I felt – unusually, for me – very nervous. I was relaxing in my bedroom, concentrating on the arias I would be singing and trying to relieve my tension, when suddenly there were several rings of the doorbell interspersed with animated voices and shrieks of laughter. I called Maya and asked what was happening, and she replied in a very condescending way that she had invited some of her friends, who were coming to the concert, for drinks. There was nothing I could do: the harm had already been done, and my longed-for peace had been shattered. Maya went back to her guests, saying loudly that I, as always, disapproved and was making a fuss about nothing.

In my early days on tour during the war, I took only the bare necessities in the way of clothes, leaving my one Sunday best outfit at home in my bedroom wardrobe. Clothes were, in any case, very thin on the ground for someone such as I. At weekends, after I had returned to London, I would often participate in 'pupil concerts' at the home of my teacher, Manlio Di Veroli; and reaching in the wardrobe for my one Sunday dress or suit, I would find an empty space. On being asked if she had seen the article in question, Maya would reply very patronizingly, 'Yes. I went out the other evening and wore it. When I bent down to pick something up, the skirt split right across. It was too *tight* for me.' This was always said in an accusatory tone, with no apology. There was no recompense, simply anger at my being slimmer than she.

In the end I was forced to travel with my entire possessions, for time and time again I would discover a handbag, a pair of shoes, or books missing, and Maya's reply would always be, '*You* weren't using them, so I gave them away.' To whom? It was useless to ask, or to remonstrate with her. As far as she was concerned, she had acted entirely logically, and therefore no argument would make the slightest bit of difference.

One day during her housekeeping period, while I was at home and needed to do some ironing, I could not find the iron or ironing board. I searched everywhere, and as Maya was out, I had no choice but to look in her room. I preferred never to do this, as the room was completely chaotic. But there was the iron and ironing board, covered in a heap of odds and ends, including papers and letters. As I went to lift off this mess, my eye fell on a letter that had obviously been typed by my father. I recognized my name and Gene's on the page – it was a reply to a letter Maya had sent Father, and it corroborated whatever appalling things she had written to him about Gene and me.

On her return, I confronted her with the letter and suggested that if it replied to remarks she had made, it would be better for her to leave, there and then, as we were obviously undesirable to her. Naturally, I was accused of spying on her by searching through her personal effects. She did eventually leave, but only in her own time. For a long period after that, there was no contact between us and my life returned to a fairly even keel. Father had, of course, sided with her, and so I was free of him, too, for a while.

A few years later, when Gene and I had returned from the States and were living in Queens Gate, Maya and I returned to a 'skating on ice' sort of relationship. Several further incidents similar to those described above took place. At one point, a doctor prescribed certain injections for a vocal problem I was experiencing, and I needed a nurse to administer them. I naturally turned to Maya as a solution. She agreed to help, but charged me two guineas per injection plus the cost of the new hypodermic syringe she had bought – which she then kept for herself. However, whenever *she* was in trouble she expected me to bail her out. And, true to pattern (governed by my mortal fear and my sense of responsibility towards her), I always did.

There were times when, after one of my performances that, unbeknown to me, she had attended, I would take a taxi home to Queen's Gate and would see Maya waiting for a bus to go to *her* home. We simply ignored each other, because this is how she wanted it. Then, after a longer than usual period of silence between us, she suddenly rang me one Saturday morning, just as I was getting ready to sing a matinée of *Tosca* at Croydon. In a rather dictatorial voice she said, 'I'm just ringing to tell you that I've married', and put the receiver down, leaving me open-mouthed. I was also left with the feeling that I ought to do something conciliatory, so I rushed off to buy her a wedding present from a nearby shop *en route* to Croydon.

Her husband, Misha, turned out to be a Russian KGB defector and head of Soviet radio's propaganda station in Munich. She had met him at some Russian venues in London and had fallen for him lock, stock and barrel. He, having apparently had enough of the Soviets, had decided to seek asylum in London. Fourteen years her junior, and both dynamic and manipulative, he obviously saw in her a British passport within easy reach, supposedly giving him the right to stay in this country. But he was also a married man, with a wife and two children in Russia, and was an alcoholic.

At this particular time Maya was working for a very hush-hush department of the Foreign Office, dealing with Slavonic repatriation. Married women were not then accepted as civil servants, so, on Maya's announcement to her bosses, 'I've just got married – and guess to whom!', she was met with a momentary silence before being shown the door in no uncertain manner. This, of course, totally unbalanced her. And from that moment on, Maya was a person under observation: her telephone was bugged, and an officer from the CID patrolled the pavements outside her flat for twenty-four hours a day.

In 1955 she and Misha were entertaining one of his ex-KGB buddies for a weekend. By a coincidence, he came from the same grim little village outside Moscow – Leonosovo – where, as children, we had spent so many formative months. On this particular Saturday morning he went out somewhere, saying that he would be back in the evening. Early that afternoon there was a phone call for Maya from Scotland Yard, asking her whether she and her husband knew someone of his name. 'Oh yes', she cheerfully replied, 'he's staying with us. He's out at the moment, but he'll be back this evening.' An acerbic voice then told her, 'Just for the record, you may be interested to know that he's just embarked on a Soviet ship at Liverpool.' He was a double agent.

From then on, vigilance of the *ménage à deux* in West Kensington was intensified, as was the apparent pace of their lives. Friends who visited them were dismayed at the amount of vodka being consumed, and those who stayed for weekends found the drink at the top of the menu at breakfast-time. Soon afterwards, the powers-that-be tactfully suggested that the time had come for the couple to move to greener pastures, suggesting that Canada would be ideal. They were therefore asked to prepare for a journey, the date and destination of which would be arranged for them. The destination turned out to be Toronto where, it was promised, they would be met by a representative who would provide them with accommodation, cash and a job for each of them. Since they would be travelling by boat, they could take a certain amount of possessions with them.

Because of these rather overwhelming circumstances, Maya and I had made an uneasy truce. The shock of being forced out of her home and country and into a nebulous future – with a possibly dangerous spouse – was making her rather twitchy. After all, no one – Maya least of all – could be sure that Misha was not himself a double agent. As usual, she was without a penny, having been out of work and with a husband to feed. I helped her as much as I could by lending her a sum of money – more than I could really afford – to tide her over. As always, my help was taken completely for granted. When she and Misha arrived in Toronto, there was no one to meet them, no accommodation, no cash and no job. They were on their own. Luckily, it was not long before they were able to start a new life there – Misha had trained as a heating and refrigeration engineer before joining the KGB, and Maya had both her linguistic ability and her bossy organizing talents!

I heard rumours from over the ocean – of drunken binges, bashings and screaming rows – and all the time, the monitoring continued, this time in the shape of the Royal Canadian Mounted Police. When Misha was drunk he had a nasty habit of making his way to the nearest Soviet embassy or consulate to give himself up, so the Mounties had quite a task on their hands. The couple also made friends with Victor Kravchenko, author of the famous book *I Chose Freedom*, who never, ever ventured outside his front door without wearing a mask. I once had the dubious pleasure of meeting him at Maya's apartment, an encounter that left me feeling very uneasy.

In 1957 I was left alone and penniless on Gene's death. Maya's only response was to tell me that if she could have helped me she would have done so. Then she played a nasty trick on me. She wrote to say that the only way in which she could help was for me to give up my flat in Queen's Gate and to come to Toronto, where she and Misha would be delighted to put me up and to help me financially until I found my own feet, which would not take long. For the first time in my relationship with Maya I genuinely thought she intended to help me – mainly, I think, because the solution seemed so logical. After all, there could be an enormous opening for an experienced singer in Canada, and of course the USA was very close. I therefore accepted Maya's suggestion as the godsend I had been waiting for, and went ahead with the arrangements.

One day I went to visit a mutual friend and told her about the miracle that had just fallen into my lap. She went pale and said, 'Forgive me for what I'm about to show you, but although I would *never* break the confidence of either you or Maya, I *have* to show you this letter from her. Otherwise I would never forgive myself.' The letter stated very bluntly that Maya and Misha were shattered by the fact that *I* had suggested coming to live with them. Neither of them wanted me, they had no spare room for me and not in their wildest dreams could they support me until I was independent. I was extremely grateful to my friend. Had she not given me this warning I would have been catapulted into my biggest ever disaster. However, I never let Maya know the reason why I suddenly changed my mind about going to Canada.

Her marriage to Misha was rapidly disintegrating, and by the time I went to New York with the Players Theatre in 1961 she was in a hysterical state. No sooner had I arrived at my hotel than I received a frantic phone call from her. She was threatening suicide if I did not go to her at once. Misha had left her, and she was uncontrollable. He had apparently acquired a girlfriend and, returning home drunk one night, found all his belongings thrown out onto the veranda of their apartment. Maya naturally expected pleadings and reconciliations from him, instead of which he picked up his belongings and drove off to the girlfriend. And stayed there. By this time, his health had collapsed and he was an extremely sick man. Now having no control over, or even contact with, him, Maya had gone berserk.

As this was on a Friday and we were not starting rehearsals until the Monday, I took the night train to Toronto – idiot that I was. Instead of welcoming my visit (we had not seen each other for more than five years) Maya stormed around, trashing Misha, calling the girlfriend a whore, and attacking *me* verbally – as only she could. *She* was the victim, and once again it was everybody else's fault, including mine. Her behaviour towards me was so terrifying that I had no choice but to beat a hasty retreat to a hotel on my last night in Toronto. I had a very demanding contract to fulfil in New York, and I had to be sane in order to do it. As always, Maya begged my forgiveness and swore that she would make up for her behaviour towards me.

However, I had no peace in New York because she was always on the phone, threatening this, that, and the other, and always ending with a suicidal postscript. Eventually, after a long season with The Strollers in East 54th Street, I could stand the strain no longer, and gave in my notice. I went back to Toronto, thinking that, in addition to providing company for Maya, I could establish myself as a singer in what seemed like a country full of opportunities. Once again, I was wrong. Maya made my life such hell that my nerves were shattered and what little ego I still had quickly disappeared. Any attempt on my part to make contact with the musical world was baulked by her, and whenever she could, she would trot out her favourite insult: 'You're not Tosca now, you're not on the stage anymore.'

Soon after my arrival in Toronto, news came that Misha was gravely ill with cyrrhosis of the liver and had been rushed to hospital. So, in addition to being at Maya's beck and call, I also had to visit the hospital in an adjoining town at her behest, as a go-between. In the end she joined me in a visit to the hospital and demanded to see him. As always, I was sent in ahead to his room as an envoy. He was wired-up and unrecognizable, and begged me piteously to prevent Maya from seeing him. He explained that he had had enough and could not bear to see her again.

By now, Maya had been informed by the nursing sister that she was not a welcome visitor. When I tactfully relayed Misha's message to her she started raving, and screamed, 'I am his wife, and I have the *right* to see him.' In a rage, she swept out of the room and down the corridor, pushing aside anyone who tried to restrain her. She hurled herself into Misha's room and slammed the door behind her. After a few minutes she was physically hauled out by hospital staff. It was not long afterwards that Misha died. Returning to Toronto, Maya collapsed and seemed incapable of any actions or decisions, so it fell to me to make all the funeral arrangements. I even had to contact Misha's girlfriend to ask for a suit of clothes for his body. Maya did not lift a finger, except to criticize me.

Through having to contact their friends and business associates I was appalled by what I learned of their relationship and way of life. Misha had previously been a partner in a very up-and-coming engineering firm, and the other partners had managed to buy houses for themselves and were living quite prosperously. But he and Maya lived in a small, squalid bed-sit – between them, they had smoked and drunk all their money away.

It was a cold spring in Toronto, and now her central heating was on full-blast. I had always loathed central heating, and slept with a window open, no matter where I was; here, I was suffocating. My throat was dry, and my tonsils started to swell. At about this time I had an audition with the director of the then embryonic Canadian Opera Company, and begged Maya to turn the heating off, at least temporarily. Her reply was, 'It is I who matters, not you.' I went to the audition knowing that I was below par, and for the first time in my life I did not do myself justice. The audition was a dead loss. From then onwards I gave up all attempts at making further musical contacts in Toronto, and I did not even approach the Canadian Broadcasting Corporation or any agents. Maya had won.

Sleeping in the same room as Maya was destroying my health, and I soon had no choice but to move into a bedsit of my own nearby. She then asked me to find *her* a new flat, and I did so, moving her into it and doing all I could to make her a comfortable new home. But the money I had saved in New York had by now trickled away, and I realized that I had to return to London. Coincidentally, friends had written to tell me that Seva, the boyfriend I had left behind, was again feeling very unwell and that I ought to return to help him. This is what I did – against Maya's pleadings and threats. She prophesied that within five years she would be dead from cancer, and she was to be proved correct – almost as if, by wishful thinking, she were punishing all those wrongdoers who had ruined her life.

In 1965 a mutual friend rang me from Toronto to tell me that Maya had been unwell and had been diagnosed with cancer of the lungs. (For as long as I can remember, she had smoked sixty fags a day.) I immediately left my job at the BBC, arranged an overdraft with my bank, and rushed off to Canada. Maya's condition had in no way softened her attitude towards me, and she was more aggressive and dictatorial than ever before. Now, it was my health that she resented. I could stay with her only a couple of weeks, and soon after my return home she came to London in the hope of finding more hopeful medical advice. But the verdict was the same. She therefore returned to Toronto to tie up any loose ends and to dispose of her effects, and then came back to London await the end.

Five years earlier I had taken over our family's old flat in West Kensington, which Maya had been renting to some very irresponsible tenants. It was in an appalling condition, and I had therefore redecorated and furnished it as best I could on my very limited resources. This, of course, added even further to Maya's rage and resentment. After staying with me in the flat for a few weeks she went to St Mary's Hospital, Paddington, and shortly afterwards into a hospice for the terminally ill. For the past year I had given up all my temping work so that I could devote my whole time and energies to her. I was existing on a social welfare sickness payment of six pounds per week – a pittance even then – but somehow I managed. Maya and I had now reached a silent truce; I bore her no grudge, and, apart from sadness at the knowledge that no reconciliation between us had lasted more than a few minutes, I had none of the usual regrets at not having done my best for her. I felt I had done all I possibly could, and at times far more than I need have done.

Maya died very peacefully in March 1967. It was a wonderful spring, and I had surrounded her with flowers until the end. She had bequeathed her body for medical research but, cancer-ridden, it was unfortunately rejected by the hospital authorities. She had vehemently demanded no religious ceremony, and in this, too, her wishes were not fulfilled. For the sake of her friends, many of whom were religious, I arranged a small church funeral and then scattered her ashes near my mother's grave in Mortlake cemetery.

After the funeral, when everyone had gone home, my old friend Princess Xenia stayed behind to keep me company. We were standing and chatting animatedly when, without warning, my skirt started to unfasten of its own accord before sliding very slowly to the ground, leaving me looking utterly ridiculous. We burst out laughing and, in one of those moments when two people say the same thing at the same time, we both remarked, 'Maya's here!'

✻

Now, for the first time in my life, I was on my own and free from destructive responsibilities. I would no longer be forced to destroy myself through other people's demands or mistakes, and the mistakes would now be my own. But on Maya's demise I was once again literally penniless, with a big overdraft. My health had also suffered very badly from the continual strain I had been under. I had a complete medical overhaul that involved surgery, and once I was more or less back to normal health, I started my life again from scratch.

There had been countless troublesome episodes involving my sister. In recalling some of them in this chapter, my intention has been not to castigate her but merely to remember things as they were and how badly they affected me. As I do so, I realize that in Maya's own mind she was right. To her, therefore, all her actions were justified. That is the way she saw things, and that is the way they were.

38

Return to Russia

IN 1968, on the first anniversary of Maya's death, I was visited by a high-ranking member of the International Red Cross who, at the request of my half-sister Alice in Moscow, had spent quite some time trying to locate me. Contact between my family and Alice had been abruptly severed at the moment war was declared in 1939, and it never occurred to me that we would find each other again. At that time, contact with Russia was not something to be undertaken lightly, for the dangers to both parties were enormous.

Within a few days of this visit I received my first letter from Alice, and its emotional impact on me was enormous. In my reply I had to admit, very sadly, that I was the only remaining member of our family. I also sent her many photographs. Alice was then sixty-eight years old, and a short while afterwards I decided to take the enormous risk of visiting her, even though this was long before such visits were practicable or even approved of. I managed to obtain a visa and a plane ticket, but on the day before my departure I learned that the Soviets had invaded Czechoslovakia. In despair, I rang the Foreign Office for advice and was told that I would be going to Moscow at my own risk. Once I touched Russian soil, I would automatically become a Soviet citizen, having been born in Russia, and the British authorities would then have no jurisdiction over me. Anything could happen to me. So that was that.

Some time afterwards Alice listened to my pleadings for her to try to visit me, and applied for a visa to come to London. The procedure dragged on and on, and eventually her request was refused: firstly, because of her age; and secondly, because she regularly took sleeping tablets – no one on any form of medication whatsoever was allowed out of Russia. I never saw her again, for it was not until 1975, when I was fifty-nine, that I returned to my native land. By then, she had died of cancer, and I had been corresponding with her sixteen year-old granddaughter Irina, the daughter of her son Igor.

Irina and Igor had arranged to meet me at the airport in Moscow, but on my arrival, passport and luggage proceedings took much longer than normal. We were made to feel insecure and nervous, and every passport was chewed over a dozen times, as if the officials were searching for a murderer or a spy. When my turn eventually came, my passport was toothcombed – upside down and inside out, raised to the light, and so on – by two young, loutish-looking soldiers. Finally, one of them snapped it shut and returned it to me. Assuming that I understood no Russian, he smirked and said to his colleague the vernacular equivalent of 'Blimey! She must have been a stunner when she was young!' Their reaction to my response in perfect Russian – 'You're quite right; I think I was' – was spectacular.

After a lengthy and exhausting battle to reclaim my luggage, I found myself in the reception area. By this time the crowd had thinned out, and I caught my first glimpse of Irina. It was deeply touching. She was sitting on a bench, looking forlorn, her head hanging low and her arms flopping limply, clutching a sadly fading bunch of flowers. When I shook her shoulder slightly, she jumped with a start. The excitement, the tension, and the endless waiting had gradually broken down her defences, and she burst into tears. But after we had embraced for a few moments, she was beaming. Having found her father Igor, my nephew, we stepped out into the Moscow sunshine. It is impossible to describe my feelings, knowing that this was Russia – *my* Russia – and that I was walking on its hallowed ground.

In the mid-1970s it was still forbidden to stay anywhere but the nominated hotel, so that is where we all got off our bus. I was staying at the Hotel Metropole, at that time a superb time capsule of bygone luxury and good taste. I understand that it has now become one of the most expensive hotels in the world. Irina and Igor were not allowed upstairs to my room, and I could feel the fear that ran through them. All hotels were *out of bounds to Russians* – in their own country! To me this was unimaginable, but they seemed to take it completely for granted. So began my first visit to a country that was very near to me and yet so far away.

Irina was extraordinarily good-looking, with an individual style, and she was dressed mostly in what I had been sending her over the years. Together, we stood out like sore thumbs and made a striking pair. I was very conscious of being under official surveillance, but was determined to see as much of my relatives as of Moscow itself. My first visit to their flat in the heart of the sprawling city was very emotional for all of us. To them, it was an amazing experience to have, for the first time, a visitor from a forbidden world; for me, to see inside a private home was almost traumatic, because I realized that it was a privilege denied to so many other visitors.

Igor, his wife Tatyana, her mother, and Irina lived in a flat that was like thousands of others in Moscow: two small rooms, a smaller, walk-through room, a tiny kitchen and an even tinier bathroom. For everyone lucky enough to have a flat, rather than a single room in a communal establishment, this was the pattern of accommodation – so many square feet allocated per person. Although the family had the unusual luxury of two and a half rooms for four people, the furniture was very basic – just the bare necessities, with a divan bed in every room. Wherever I went in the city, it was duplicated exactly, even down to the colours of the furniture.

Until very recently the Russian people had had no access to foreigners or the foreign media, and they had been brainwashed into believing totally that their own country was paradise and that everywhere else was hell. One of the first questions that Tatyana asked me was, 'How do our living conditions compare with yours?' While asking this, she was almost bursting with pride, and so I had to be very gentle and tactful in my reply. However, the table was laden with delectable food – almost anachronistically so – and again, I was to encounter this wherever I went in Moscow.

Before long we were relaxed and conversing on a number of subjects, and I remember saying something to the effect that I could not judge a certain situation because I had never known a lack of freedom. To this, Tatyana remarked wistfully, 'I, of course, have never known freedom.' These words seared into me and have remained with me ever since. Whenever the phone rang, everybody froze with fear; the phone was mostly the bringer of bad tidings, and even arrests were made by telephone. Igor was a geologist, digging for oil in Siberia, and was on leave from his job, but Tatyana worked all day on some hush-hush job that made her very vulnerable. I admired her for her courage in inviting me to their home – against great odds. When I mentioned this to her, she replied that my visit was worth *any* risk.

Fortunately, nothing really went wrong during my visit, and I was able to see a lot of Moscow and its outskirts with either Igor or Irina. It was early autumn, and one day as I set off to meet Irina across Red Square, I was waylaid by a 'midnight cowboy' as I stepped out of my hotel. Waiting to pick up wealthy foreign ladies, he preened himself to impress me and looked me up and down. Then he began to look concerned, and said, 'Why are you so lightly dressed? You'll catch your death of cold! Go and change.' I laughed and walked on, relieved at this turn of events.

Across Red Square was an immense, labyrinthine, modern building called the Hotel Moskva, and I was amused when told later that during the building excavations, huge caches of jewellery and valuables had been found buried in what were once private gardens. They had been hidden by wealthy families at the beginning of the Revolution, and they virtually paid for the construction of the whole building.

After a week in Moscow Igor, Irina and I went off to St Petersburg – then still known as Leningrad. It was a full day's journey by train, but as sitting together was taboo, our meetings took place by appointment in corridors or toilets. On arrival we were again forced to part company; as usual, I went off to my hotel, while the others went to the friends with whom they were staying. The following morning we almost failed to meet up at my hotel, because it was chock-a-block with tourists and I did not realize that we were known to the staff by number rather than by name. Somehow or other, Irina eventually caught a glimpse of me and we were reunited.

That evening we dropped in to the Mariinski Theatre where an opera was in progress. All I wanted was to see the foyer and feel the atmosphere of the place, but an usher seemed to sense that I was somehow 'special' and asked us what we were doing there. When I told her, she led us to the Tsar's box, still as beautiful as it must have been when it was built. By now the first half of the opera had finished, and she politely asked the people sitting in the box to vacate it for the interval so that we could enjoy to the full the few minutes at our disposal. I had many such experiences in Russia that filled me with both joy and grief – at the goodness and kindness of the person in the street, in a country capable of such incredible horrors.

Although I always dress simply, something about my appearance is individual, and everyone in Leningrad who saw me took me for what I was: a White Russian returning as a sightseer. This added great magic to my visit. It seemed as if all doors were open to me; all I had to do was smile. I remember finding a still-functioning church and longing to feel the atmosphere of a service in progress, rather than admiring the mere shells of so many churches that had been used as meat depots or something equally sacrilegious. I therefore went inside with Irina, and as we passed a group of worshippers I heard one of them say, 'Oh look! She must be an actress – from Paris, probably.'

Between 1975 and 1992 I visited Russia five times, and on each visit, incidents similar to that mentioned above took place. During a trip to the Tsarskoe Selo, Irina and I were forced to join an immense queue, but suddenly an usher singled me out, saying, 'Come with me.' She led us round to the exit at the back of the palace and, embracing me, said, 'I hate the thought of you waiting for hours. Go in through the back.' We therefore saw the exhibition in reverse order.

When touring the Tretikoff Gallery with the curator, who is a friend of mine, the ushers nudged each other and murmured, 'She must be a Romanov.' My St Petersburg accent beguiled everyone with its upper-class vagaries and vernacular, and hotel receptionists would engage me in long conversations simply to hear something that they had only vaguely imagined. In a theatre that I was visiting, a man tapped me on the shoulder and asked, 'Excuse me, but are you an aristocrat?' When I replied, 'Not at all, I come from the intelligentsia', he said in desperation, 'Oh, but you *must* be an aristocrat. This is how we imagine them to look.'

Visiting the lovely gardens surrounding a great cathedral in Moscow, I sat in the sunshine, meditating, and was disturbed by shouting and cursing across the small piazza. A bag lady, big and chunky, was roughly shaking an old vagrant who was doubtless sleeping off whatever he had recently imbibed while resting his head on a loosely-filled plastic bag. She screamed at him, 'This is God's corner! How *dare* you lie there like that, you drunken bastard! Get up! Go to the railway station and join all the other homeless louts! Go on, get going!' He tried to fend her off, but kept falling back onto his 'pillow'.

After a while I had had enough of this and went over to them, peremptorily telling her to stop molesting the old man. It was none of her business, I pointed out. She stood up, hands on hips, looked me up and down disgustedly, and shouted, 'What the hell do you know about this, you overpainted whore, all cosseted and covered in gold? Mind your own bloody business!' I dutifully retreated, and when I last saw the couple they were sitting together and dozing cosily, her head on his shoulder.

39

St Petersburg Stories

O N ONE OF MY TRIPS to 'Peter's City' I visited the celebrated Alexander Nevsky monastery and cemetery. The latter is mind-boggling in its wealth of famous 'residents'. Composers, writers, artists are all segregated in their relevant plots, and the visitor is both overwhelmed by the familiarity of their names and awe-inspired by their past greatness. The cemetery feels like a secret world, one that brings a reminder of the inevitability of mortality.

After my visit I had to sit down and think for a while, and so I chose the café of a large hotel nearby. As I sat ruminating, I suddenly heard the sound of cockney being spoken near me and saw a small group of young girls walking in my direction. I stopped the leader and asked her what they, a group of London teenagers, were doing in St Petersburg. 'We're studyin' Russian in Kiev', came her reply. This suggested an encouraging degree of dedication and broadening of cultural horizons, and I asked her how she felt about the language she was learning. 'Well, iss differen', innit?' End of conversation!

I have often wondered whether her Russian vocabulary became as colourful as her English.

*

One of the most amazing innovations, if such it can be called, that I discovered when shopping in Russia was the procedure devised for purchasing even the simplest commodity such as a loaf of bread or a slab of butter – if these were available, of course. First, one had to queue for as long as twenty minutes to obtain a chit for the goods to be paid for; with this chit, one queued for another fifteen or twenty minutes to pay for the produce; and then one returned to the original queue for another long period in order to claim the purchase with the paid-up chit. This was bad enough for me as a tourist, but even worse for local workers who spent their entire lunch break, and sometimes even longer, in buying just one or two commodities.

Another oddity was that one could thumb down any passing car as a taxi, without fear of being robbed, mugged or raped. This was a great convenience, providing that one had the cash (in dollars or sterling) to pay for it.

✳

My penultimate visit to St Petersburg took place during the season of the White Nights, which was quite magical. Staying in a hotel on the waterfront, I would often go out late at night with several 'pussy bags' and feed the stray cats: an unspeakable joy to be doing something so peaceful and quiet and so dear to me. This was in the days before the mafia arrived, when the city was still safe, and I would wander for long periods without fear or nervousness, returning to my hotel at one or two in the morning, just as the magical sun was sinking very slowly in a golden haze.

✳

My last trip to Russia, in 1992, had some extremely poignant moments. On the side wall of a very imposing building at the upper end of the Nevsky Prospect in St Petersburg I suddenly caught sight of an inscription, dating back perhaps a hundred years, that read: BRANDT'S BANK. I realized at once that this very building was where my father had spent his apprenticeship before travelling to England at the beginning of the century to take a job at the bank's London branch.

I also saw that the original Fabergé building and shop, once disguised as a money-lending centre with the pawnbroker's three golden balls very much in evidence, had now been returned to its original splendour. The interior was superb – pure art deco, looking much as it must have done in the building's heyday. A grocery, famous in my mother's day and familiar to me because of this, had had its splendid art deco similarly restored – a perfect cameo frozen in time.

I returned from St Petersburg via Riga to stay with my great friend Richard Samuel, then the British ambassador in Latvia. I took a risk and travelled by train, having a carriage to myself. This, I must admit, was very eerie; and although I tried not to panic, I felt extremely vulnerable. The train stopped many times in the middle of nowhere, and then I heard loud whispering and lots of running up and down in and around the carriages.

We were due to arrive in Riga at about eight in the morning and, having had practically no sleep at all, I ventured into the toilet to wash, only to find the low floor submerged in inches of urine that was by now lapping over onto the floor of the corridor. I had no choice but to step in and wade through it in order to meet my own call of nature and then get to the tap – which I discovered to be dry! I slunk back to my compartment and dressed as best I could, covering myself in layers of perfume, ready for Richard to meet me.

40

Basil Merriman

A MONG THE EXTRAORDINARY episodes in my life that actually bore no relevance to my artistic career, one of the oddest was my meeting with Basil Merriman in 1937, when I was twenty-one. One evening a girlfriend and I had gone to see a film in the West End, and as she lived just off Park Lane I decided to walk her home before going back to the family flat in West Kensington. As we were walking down Piccadilly I became conscious that we were being followed, and we hastened our steps accordingly. I felt certain that whoever was following us had hastened theirs as well, so I casually looked behind me and saw two elegantly dressed young men who were obviously keeping pace with us.

A few minutes later the two men overtook us, and one of them very politely accosted us, concentrating on me. He would not accept our refusal of his offer of a coffee or supper, and when the confrontation became rather heated the less vociferous young man decided to leave. The other remained and made it quite clear that he had no intention of giving up the fight, saying that if I allowed him to walk my friend home with me, he would then escort me to *my* home. All our attempts to get away from him seemed futile. I even threatened to scream for a policeman, but he told me that if I did, he would make sure that the officer did not believe me – on the contrary, in fact.

By this time a strange feeling of adventure had taken over, and I decided to play along with him. After we had seen my friend to her door the man hailed a taxi, asking me to give my address, which was then in Challoner Crescent near West Kensington station. I did not, of course, reveal the number of the house. He then introduced himself as Dr Basil Merriman. He was extremely presentable, expensively dressed and beautifully spoken. And he had the gift of the gab. His blarney was extremely interesting and amusing, and it had definitely caught my imagination.

When we arrived at Challoner Crescent I did not invite him indoors (Mother and Maya, with whom I shared the flat, were away) but said that I had to walk my dog – my beautiful spaniel Aryk (Kyra spelt backwards) who had been given to me on my twenty-first birthday and whom I worshipped. Our walk lasted into the small hours, and despite Basil's insistent requests I would not give in and allow him in for coffee. There was something about him that I did not quite take to, even though it was difficult to pinpoint, and eventually we said goodbye and parted without commitment on either side.

A few evenings later, I was visiting my next door neighbours when their doorbell rang and I heard Maya's voice anxiously asking to speak to me. When I went to the door she explained that a young man called Basil Merriman had turned up and said that he needed to see me urgently. He was waiting for me outside our front door. I apologized to my neighbours, went outside, and found Basil in a state of extreme agitation. He kept repeating that he needed to talk to me on my own, on a matter of great urgency. It now looked as if he might become a real nuisance, and so I decided to let him have his way. He suggested that we go for a walk, and I agreed.

As we walked towards Olympia he kept up a non-stop conversation, one that initially appeared fascinating but which in reality was virtually meaningless. We reached Sinclair Road where, apparently, he lived, and he invited me in for a coffee. For some reason I felt it was easier to agree than to refuse. We entered a very large Victorian terraced house, about five storeys high, that was very dark and still inside – rather eerily so. By now I was beginning to feel extremely nervous, but I would not allow him to see this. We climbed to the third floor, entered a spacious room that was sparsely furnished and not very cosy, and Basil offered me a drink. What he said next suddenly began to make the context of our meetings take shape.

It transpired that our first meeting had not been a chance one. He had known whom he was trailing, and had followed me according to a plan. He seemed to know all about me – my family, my professional activities, in fact my whole way of life – and I learned that the object of the exercise was to persuade me to become a spy (I presumed this would be for Britain, but learned later that it would be more for Germany). I would be given a course in Russian shorthand and would be sent to Moscow as a secretary to the British Embassy. Obviously, my name would be changed. Meanwhile, it would be assumed that I had gone to Italy to study singing. I would have an 'official' address there, and in order to complete the delusion, all my correspondence would be sent back to England via Italy.

Basil reassured me that should anything untoward happen to me during my sojourn in Russia, my family would be looked after financially. While he talked, he kept fidgeting with a small radio, which was obviously tuned to a foreign station – the language being broadcast was German, and it sounded rather heated. I suddenly remembered the newspaper headlines and stories about a young woman who had acted as a spy in Russia and, having completed her duties in Moscow, was flying home to London; she was thrown out of the plane and fell to her death. This took place a few years after I came to London, and the unimaginable horror of her fall had remained with me all these years.

Basil asked for my decision, adding that the matter was very urgent. I told him in no uncertain terms to stop all such nonsense, that I had had enough, and that I wished to go home. He then produced a hypodermic syringe and threatened me with it; but whatever panic I felt inwardly, I had somehow appeared to keep my cool, and I suppose this threw him. After he had tried once more to persuade me and failed, his voice and personality changed immediately – he became the Basil Merriman I had first encountered in the street.

He escorted me downstairs, called a taxi, and said most authoritatively that what had just passed between us was now in the past and should never be mentioned again. He warned me that, since from now onwards I would be under observation, I was *never* to talk about what had happened – to *anyone*. If I did, I would regret it. He then accompanied me home, now in his 'old' personality and using his non-stop banter as conversation.

Whether this whole situation was for real, or some elaborate scenario that he had invented for kicks, I shall never really know. The subject was never again mentioned by either of us during the many times we met. But my curiosity was aroused, and after getting hold of a medical *Who's Who* I found his name easily. His entry was very long and awe-inspiring, and among his many achievements was a visit to Berlin to privately attend Hitler, who had suffered from vocal and sinus trouble – at that time, Basil was an Ear, Nose and Throat specialist.

Soon afterwards my family and I moved to a flat only a few streets away from his Sinclair Road address, and from time to time he would call without warning, always expecting me to be at his disposal. And often, when I was appearing in Variety at some theatre in London, I would find a card from him at the end of the show saying that he would be waiting for me at the stage door. On one of his visits to my home he became very obstreperous as the evening progressed, and made a serious pass at me. I suggested that he leave, but he refused and screamed that he would not go until I had succumbed to his advances. I handed him a blanket, told him to make himself comfortable on the sofa, and went to bed, locking my door behind me. In the morning he was gone.

When my career took off, Basil and I lost touch, and we did not meet again until 1974. I was on the tube to Marble Arch, where I worked as a secretary in a nearby tapestry gallery, and he got on the train at Holland Park, where he now lived, and sat beside me. Although he was still doing valuable work in practice and research, he had obviously become an alcoholic, however hard he tried to conceal the fact. His mind still intrigued me, but he had become boring without acquiring any other qualities to compensate for it. Our relationship returned to how it had once been: sporadic and leading nowhere.

One day he arrived *chez moi* plastered beyond disguise, trying to hide his weakness by denigrating me. Having expressed vociferously what a bore he now was, I showed him the door, and that was that. We occasionally bumped into each other at the local supermarket, but by then he was almost unrecognizable.

41

A New Career

B Y 1972 I had still not completely adjusted to my rather barren
new life, and somehow the things that most perpetuated the
problem were my memorabilia and my piano. It seemed as if they
and I could not live together, and I felt I had to rid myself of everything that had been part of my past life as a singer. The process,
though painful, did not take long to complete.

My costumes went to an amateur theatre company attached to a
hospital, and as my sheet music had been turned down by most of
the London music colleges because it was not completely pristine, I
divided it between two aspiring singers. My jewellery and superb
stage regalia, which would now be worth a considerable sum, went
via an acquaintance to the Royal Opera House, Covent Garden, for
thirty-five pounds. This even included the wonderful *Tosca* ring that
Mary Garden had given me. The money was not important, however, and I was glad that the Covent Garden museum would make
use of all the jewellery.

The last thing to be disposed of was my piano, and this was
given to the local branch of the Royal National Institute for the
Blind. It is hard to explain my feeling of liberation as I saw the
piano disappear through the back garden gate; but I had an overwhelming sensation of freedom at being able to start a new life
with no shackles.

Although I had thrown away bag upon bag of photos, reviews
and publicity material, something stopped me from disposing of
absolutely everything. I therefore kept a nucleus, covering a long
period of my singing career, and hid this away deep in a seldom-
visited cupboard. Meanwhile, my recorded tapes and acetates dating back to 1935 were piled in a cardboard box under the bed in my
spare room. What power stayed my hand from clearing out this
material too? I shall never know.

In 1981, when I was sixty-five, my office work dried up and I
faced a bleak future, financially and personally. By chance a friend
mentioned a wonderful psychic who read palms, tarot cards, and so
on, and who came up with amazing knowledge of one's past and
future. When I went to see him, he gave me a pretty concise sum-
mary of my life and said that I was not to worry since I would soon

find an activity in something that was almost unknown to most people. I had no clue as to what he was referring, and felt inclined to write it off as something simply theoretical.

Shortly afterwards, having too much time on my hands, I decided to take up portraiture at the nearby Addison Institute for Adult Education. I had always had a leaning towards art, and portraiture was of great interest to me. I commenced enthusiastically, only to find that models were harder and harder to come by. Soon I was reduced to drawing daffodils and cauliflowers. In despair, I suddenly realized that there was also a course in ceramic restoration, something which, until then, I had thought was a technical impossibility. As I had several antique ceramic ornaments that were slightly damaged, I thought I could at least restore these. I met the teacher in question and joined the course, not really knowing what would be involved.

I took to it like a duck to water – obviously it was another of those hidden talents I knew nothing about. Within two weeks I was given damaged porcelain by a local antique dealer, and returned it within a few days, invisibly made whole. And I was paid for it! This was a wonderful experience, and I took up the craft seriously, doing many a full day's work with joy. Ceramic restoration began to take off in a big way, and I bought all the equipment necessary for working at home.

So, for about fifteen years, I was employed on something completely unknown to the average outsider. It paid for my few indulgences and luxuries, and once again I was engaged in producing 'perfection'. Even the experts found it impossible to find any trace of breakage, great or small, in the pieces I had restored. I gave up ceramics only when my voice, once again, took over my life.

42

The Rebirth

A T T H E E N D O F 1988 a neighbour, Christopher Walker – an enthusiastic 'catophile' as well as the definitive authority on all things Armenian – introduced me to two other neighbours, Gary Pulsifer and Richard Bates, who both worked in publishing. I later joined them on a delightful trip to Russia that Gary organized. Soon after our return, Gary and Richard invited me to dinner to meet some Russian guests, one of whom was the programme manager of the Russian section of the BBC's World Service. After a short chat he asked if I would be willing to give a radio interview for transmission to Russia. I told him I would be delighted, little realizing that the first seeds of my 'rebirth' had just been planted.

In January 1989 a delightful young man by the name of Boris Nadan came to interview me for the programme. He was just forty, full of contagious enthusiasm and with a very charismatic personality. He told me that the format of the programme was not dissimilar to that of *Desert Island Discs*, and explained that my old tapes, whatever was on them, would provide the musical content. He did not ask to hear any of my recordings, but instead launched straight into a series of leading questions on a number of topics, including other singers – to which I replied as tactfully as I could. When he left, he took one of my tapes and said that after editing the interview and using such music as he found of interest, he would contact me again.

At about nine o'clock that evening Boris telephoned me, his voice almost hysterical. He said that it simply was not possible that there I was, sitting in the middle of Shepherd's Bush – always a rather derogatory name for West Kensington! – with a voice so glorious. When he had first heard my old tape he had gone completely berserk; the impact of something so utterly unexpected hit him below the belt, and he said he felt he should have been warned in advance what he was going to hear.

A few days later he arrived with the edited interview. After listening to it and agreeing on its excellence – full of excitement at being involved in such a historic event, Boris had done a beautiful job – he said, 'And now you have to write a book. You *must*.' I replied that I was too old, having no more time or energy for the task, and suggested that he should write it himself. His face darkened. Looking down, he said, 'You say *you* have no time, but it's I who has none. I have about a year to live.' I got the message at once, and asked him, 'You have AIDS?' Although I knew what his answer would be, I was still shattered by it. This was my first encounter with the disease, and it hit me like a physical blow.

An extraordinary bond developed between Boris and me, and for several months we saw a tremendous amount of each other. He vowed that, even if it were the last thing he would do in his life, he would make the world hear and acknowledge my voice – it *would* be reborn. In fact he lived for a further twenty months, and he did work enormously hard to create interest in me, wherever and however he could. But, as has so often been the case in my career, numerous obstacles presented themselves. Although he wrote to every specialist recording company in England, the replies – if they came at all – were all the same: 'A great voice, but her timing is wrong. We do not issue recordings made after 1930.'

Boris battled on for me, even when his strength was waning, and somehow his enormous enthusiasm became contagious. He *made* people listen with fresh ears to the tapes, and even my close friends of many years' standing heard my voice as never before. Until then they had listened only vaguely, doubtless out of politeness, to someone whom they considered a failure. They had listened, but never actually *heard*; the tapes were the same as they had always been, yet now people looked at me with different eyes and with far greater interest. One of these listeners was Earl Okin.

I first knew of Earl when I worked as a secretary for Barclays Bank in Westbourne Grove, where his mother was one of my colleagues. He was then a schoolteacher, but in his spare time performed as an alternative comedian and jazz musician, singing and playing the piano superbly and writing his own music and lyrics. He was also a great *aficionado* of opera singers, but refused to acknowledge anyone past that magic date of 1930 – the Golden Era of singers. It took Earl's mother a long time to persuade him to listen to my tapes, but when he eventually heard them he, too, was left open-mouthed. He met Boris, and they eulogized together.

Boris was by now regressing noticeably. He gave up his job at the BBC and tried every remedy that he heard of, but all to no avail. By the beginning of 1991 he was gone, and with him all his hopes and dreams of making my voice known to the world. But by some miracle, Earl took over. Now a full-time comedian, raconteur and musician, he kept saying, 'I *know* there's something I can do to get you recognition, but I can't put my finger on what it is.' He wrote to every recording company in England, just as Boris had done, but received similarly negative replies.

Then he suddenly had a brainwave: a profile of me in the widely read *Record Collector* magazine. The article he wrote proved to be of enormous interest, and, as luck would have it, the editor then compiled a CD that included two arias by each of the artists featured in the magazine that year. He chose my recording of Jaroslavna's two magnificent arias from Borodin's *Prince Igor*, and they received remarkable acclaim. At long last, my voice had appeared on a professionally produced recording, and suddenly, from being virtually unknown, my name seemed to be on the lips of all the operaphiles.

Earl was so encouraged that when he went to Vienna in 1993 for one of his own gigs he took my tapes to Preiser, one of the most prestigious firms dealing solely with recordings of singers from the Golden Era. Otto Preiser listened to the tapes and was astonished by what he heard, remarking that although he had never heard of me or my voice, I was a great singer who belonged with the other 'Greats' of the Golden Era. Colin Tilney, my wonderful ex-accompanist, also believed that I deserved to be heard again, and he made a substantial financial contribution to the project. After cleaning the old tapes as much as was possible, Preiser released two discs of my old recordings which, to my astonishment, were highly acclaimed by all the music critics both here and in the United States.

The experiment of those two CDs paid off. Instead of a few hundred copies bought by collectors, they sold in amazing quantities. In fact, they broke all records in their field. Here, then, was the fulfilment of that prophecy made more than thirty years earlier. The media took up the story, and soon more and more people in all walks of life knew about me and the miracle that had happened to me – or, rather, to my voice. After being 'cast away' on *Desert Island Discs* I received extraordinary letters from listeners, some of whom had found my story a kind of inspiration that had given them new hope. I was deeply touched by this. I also had a letter from a schoolfriend in the 1920s who still remembered me as a new recruit in her class, shy and awkward and speaking no English.

Naturally, I received many letters from collectors and *aficionados*, and also from people who remembered my performances as far back as the 1940s. Quite a few of them were men who, in their teens, had been halberdiers in our production of *Tosca* with the Italian Opera Company. They could remember my costumes, the way I walked on stage, and in fact everything about the production – it had been their initiation into the world of grand opera. Some of them had been bowled over by my belated reappearance; they had often wondered where, having disappeared so suddenly, I had disappeared *to*, and had assumed that I had either kicked the bucket or gone abroad. In my own small way, I had become a cult figure at the age of eighty.

A number of people also wrote to say that they wished to write my biography or a play about my life. One letter in particular brought me great amusement. It was from a couple who had simply decided that they were going to write the biography of Kyra Vayne. They invited me to stay with them, giving an extraordinarily detailed description of their house that included a plan of their kitchen, the sitting-room, and so on, and adding that as they both used the shower, I could have the bathroom to myself. They would take me for walks in the countryside and deal with any dietary problems I might have. They even went so far as to give me a date that was convenient for them, confident that it would suit me as well!

I wrote back to them, saying as carefully and tactfully as I could that I was otherwise engaged for the time being. Soon afterwards I received a fairly vituperative reply that underlined my obvious ingratitude. I have often thought what a superb black comedy play this could have made – a wonderful whodunnit plot, with me as the victim . . .

However, my newfound celebrity was not all humour and happiness. Remembering how, in the early 1970s, I had disposed of all my wonderful costumes and stage jewellery and thrown away most of my memorabilia, I suddenly felt a deep sense of injury that they were no longer mine. I was also reminded that *no one* had been close enough to prevent me from acting so stupidly in giving them away. The first thing I did was to ring Covent Garden and ask what had happened to my jewellery. I was told firstly that no one remembered seeing anything that matched its description, and secondly that someone did, after all, remember it arriving but that then it disappeared and was never seen again. Although several friends also approached the Opera House on my behalf, all their efforts at locating the jewellery proved similarly futile.

At times, the irony of my new situation outweighed the joy, and I would fall into deep depression. During these periods, all I wanted was to opt out and return to the placid and plebeian life I had been living before my rebirth. And although I have made many new friends, it seems as if I have lost a few of the old ones. They have found my transition from 'nobody' to 'somebody' rather difficult to take, and have edged out of my life. But since the miracle happened and the prophecy came true, my life seems to have been bewitched. There is simply one coincidence after another – unbelievable incidents that somehow link up in a very strange way, as if some higher force were acting as a kind of magnet to bring together the debris of my life into a coherent shape.

While I was in the local supermarket the other day, my arm was suddenly grabbed by a young man who started talking excitedly to me. He knew that I was a ceramics restorer and explained that he had once come to visit me to look at my equipment. I told him that I did indeed vaguely remember him. He rambled on for a while and then asked me if I were Russian, and when I said that I was, he told me that there was a very interesting Russian lady living very nearby – just down the road, in fact – who had been an opera singer; she had appeared on *Desert Island Discs* and I absolutely *had* to meet her. When I replied that I had news for him, and that I happened to be the lady he was referring to, the information did not immediately register with him. When it eventually sank in, he almost passed out with shock.

My life also contains so many incidents that seem to have come full circle, resolving themselves, often quite unexpectedly, in the most surprising ways. For example, I had never stopped wondering what happened to the jewellery and stage regalia that I sold to the Royal Opera House, and earlier this year my good friend Mark Jones wrote to Covent Garden on my behalf to ask, yet again, of their whereabouts. Only the other day he received a reply, confirming that they had indeed been bought by the Opera House, and that, since then, they have been languishing in its archives. Never having been put on display, they have not seen the light of day for twenty-seven years. At the time of going to press, I have been told I will be reunited with them, thanks to Francesca Franchi, the archivist, and Rita Grudzien, head of publicity.

43

The Peasant Philosopher

I N 1991 an extremely pleasant interlude cheered my sunken spirits. Gary Pulsifer, then working at Peter Owen Publishers, was preparing the launch of *Laughter Over the Left Shoulder*, the autobiography of the brilliant Russian writer, Vladimir Soloukhin. As he spoke no English, Gary suggested that I be his hostess for the duration of his stay in London. For someone such as I this was quite a task to take on, but the challenge spurred me into accepting.

Awaiting Soloukhin's arrival, I conjured up an image of the man I was about to meet, but this could not have been further from reality. He was the prototype of the Russian peasant down the ages – large and clumsy, his clothes ill-fitting and crumpled, with a round, heavily-jowled face. And behind his kindly epression there lurked a gentle hint of menace. I am sure that he, in turn, must have had a mental picture of what I was going to look like, and on meeting me his surprise must have equalled mine. He later told me that he had been petrified at the thought of meeting a genuine White Russian, imagining me to appear formidable and aloof, and he was greatly relieved to find me amicable and welcoming.

Niceties over, I invited him to break bread, and before long we were getting on like a house on fire. He had a deceptively naïve and rather wily manner, together with a lively and witty sense of humour. His week's stay passed too swiftly, alas, but during that time I learned a lot about Russia – as he did about Britain – and I found his views and philosophies beguiling. He told me about the horrors of the Stalin era, and the destruction and plunder of hundreds of glorious churches, recalling how he had wandered from village to village, picking up priceless icons lying among the rubble. He was, in fact, as famous for his astonishing collection of icons as for his writing – which is saying something! (Although no one was *quite* sure as to how he came to possess this collection, he at least gloried in the history and tradition of the icons, and loved them dearly.)

We spent all our spare time talking, often well into the night, and his racy political anecdotes kept me in hysterics for hours. I also never ceased to be amused by his habit, when passing my bedroom, of peering round the door to look at my photograph, taken when I was twenty-one and wearing the bracelet given to me by Princess Andrew, while muttering to himself, 'Yes, yes ... There she is, the typical beauty ... Just the kind they looked for to send to Siberia. Ayi, ayi, ayi ... There she is.'

The book launch was a very swish affair that took place at the Soviet Embassy – still replete with portraits of Lenin and Stalin belligerently staring at people wherever they looked. It was strange, after all these years, to find myself on 'Russian territory', so to speak, yet still in my own country.

The following year, on my last visit to Moscow, Soloukhin invited me to lunch at the historic Writers' Club, a time capsule where one felt surrounded by the ghosts of all the greatest scribes of Russia. The list of members would be too long to even contemplate, and one found oneself talking in a whisper so as not to disturb their peace. He also invited me for lunch at his apartment which, in comparison to those others in Moscow I had already visited, was quite sumptuous. The walls were lined with icons of all shapes, sizes and periods, and formed a private museum. Lunch was delicious, if rather more liquid than my usual repasts. Soloukhin certainly liked his vodka, and would not take my *niets* for an answer.

As I am writing these words, I look with pleasure at the lovely icon he gave me as a souvenir of his stay in my flat. Enormously wise, he was also fortunate to possess the ambiguity necessary for living in a country such as Russia at the time that he did, while carving a name for himself. When inscribing my copy of his book he wrote, 'To the incomparable Kyra Maximovna with love, in memory of our Russia. I am so happy to have met you.' The feeling was mutual; I felt a real loss when I heard of his demise a couple of years ago, and I am privileged to have had him as a friend.

44

Recordings

FOR MANY YEARS my old tapes and acetate recordings lay forgotten in a cardboard box under the bed in my spare room,
slowly gathering dust, and I could never have imagined that they
would form the basis of my rebirth. Although they have brought
me many new friends and personal acquaintances, it is for the
benefit of the wider public, who know me only as a voice that has
been made available on CD, that I recount here the history of those
old recordings.

The first CD was released by Preiser in 1995, when I was se-
venty-nine. Jaroslavna's two arias from *Prince Igor* were recorded
on, I think, acetate at the old Levy's Studios off Baker Street in
London, and as I have already explained, they were made as audition pieces for *Kitezh* which opened the first post-war International
Opera Season at the Liceu, Barcelona. The acetate recording of
Schubert's *Im Frühling* on the same disc was made soon after private recordings became possible – this was in the late 1930s, when
I was about twenty-two and fairly raw and naïve. I made the recording simply so that I could hear my own voice, and in later years
considered it a write-off; not so the *cognoscenti*, who acclaimed my
Schubert singing as very special.

The other items on that first Preiser disc were private recordings
of radio broadcasts. The first was an orchestral concert in
Stockholm in 1959, the second a recital of Russian songs from
1965 – this was my last BBC recital, and my voice was then at its
peak. More items from this recital were included on Preiser's
second Kyra Vayne CD, which was released in 1996. The disc also
features another Stockholm radio broadcast item – Tatyana's Letter
Scene from *Eugene Onegin* – and a private studio recording of two
arias from *The Fair of Sorochintsi*, made in 1954.

The longest item on the second disc is Berlioz's *La Mort de
Cléopâtre* for soprano and orchestra. This was a private recording
of a broadcast from the BBC in Glasgow, featuring the Scottish
Radio Orchestra under Norman del Mar. My accompanist, Colin
Tilney, came across a manuscript copy of this work while brows-
ing through music in the British Museum, and suggested that I
sing it. I agreed – and became the first singer to do so. (Later,

Jennie Tourel and all the mezzo and soprano 'Greats' would take up the work). By this time I had largely abandoned my singing career and was working as a secretary, and had not sung for a long while. However, in the six weeks before the performance I was able to perfect my voice once more and to learn this long, dramatic *scena*.

Senta's ballade from *Die Fliegende Holländer*, the Bach-Gounod 'Ave Maria' and Musetta's waltz-song from *La Bohème* were all private recordings of BBC broadcasts made with Vic Oliver and his British Symphony Orchestra. The csárdás from *Die Fledermaus* also came from a BBC broadcast, while I recorded the Provost *Intermezzo* just for my own fun.

In 1996 Eklipse, too, released a CD of my old recordings. It begins with excerpts from Spontini's *La Vestale* – excerpts only, because at the beginning of the 1950s the BBC was economizing fairly drastically. No opera or operetta was played in its entirety, which explains why this particular *Vestale* is so fragmentary! The cast included Richard Lewis, Norman Lumsden, Jennifer Vivyan and Rosina Raisbeck, and was conducted by Roger Desormière.

The Miserere from *Il Trovatore*, 'Ernani, involami' from *Ernani*, and 'Vissi d'arte' from *Tosca* were all recorded from BBC broadcasts with Vic Oliver. Vic himself can be heard introducing the second and third of these items. Mussorgsky's *The Ragamuffin* and Prokofiev's *The Ugly Duckling* were recorded from BBC broadcasts in 1963; Colin Tilney was once again my accompanist. More poignant, perhaps, are the private recordings of 'Pace, pace, mio Dio' from *La Forza del Destino* and 'The Sea Without a Shore' from *Amarak*, both made at the Carnegie Hall Studios in New York in 1949. The former is the nearest I ever came to appearing at that prestigious venue, and the latter is all that remains of the musical Eugene Iskoldoff planned to put on for me. There were many beautiful songs in the show, but the project never materialized; and unfortunately all its gorgeous music was lost forever, with the exception of this one number. In fact these two recordings are all that I have to show for a particularly horrendous period in my professional life.

Adrian Foley, composer of 'One Night in Old Seville', was a friend of mine. He had a wonderful gift for writing light, lilting numbers, and the two of us recorded this one for our own mutual pleasure. Adrian was very shy, with no clout or salesmanship, and so he never achieved the success that he deserved. Later, as Lord Foley, he graced the House of Lords, but we eventually disappeared from each other's lives. He is now retired and living in great style in Marbella.

Finally, the 'Gori, Gori'/'Black Eyes' medley was recorded from another *Vic Oliver Introduces* ... programme for the BBC, of which I must have done well over a dozen. Both 'Gori, Gori' and 'Black Eyes' are very popular Russian gypsy songs, and it was this arrangement of the two numbers, made for me by Egon Stein in around 1940, that so impressed Vic when I went to audition for him.

Here I should add that while I cannot recall exactly how many broadcasts I did for the BBC, I realize that in the twenty-five years between 1940 and 1965 it must have been an enormous number. I sang for 'Auntie' under conductors that included Stanford Robinson, Anatole Fistoulari, Norman del Mar, Roger Desormière, John Pritchard, Colin Davis, Gilbert Vintner and Bruno Maderna, and these broadcasts included all types of music. But it is only recently that artists have been automatically sent a tape of their broadcasts, and since the BBC never indicated to me that copies of my own recordings might be available at the time of transmission, it did not occur to me to ask for any.

Sadly, it is now too late to put this right, because at the end of the 1960s the BBC had a huge clear-out and threw away thousands of tapes made by dozens of important artists. They kept only one recorded specimen per artist – except, of course, in the case of the real 'Greats' – and so virtually all of my broadcasts disappeared forever. I weep every time I think of this. Apart from one very mediocre tape, there is *nothing* left of the many wonderful broadcasts I took part in – the list of operas and operettas is endless. Furthermore, some of the items that I recorded for the BBC were not actually heard on air. For example, I remember giving wonderful performances of the *Vocalises* by Rachmaninov and Stravinsky that were never broadcast because my programmes overran.

Were it not for the fact that friends kindly taped some of my broadcasts and gave me copies, many of the items on my CDs would never have been heard again. My voice would have disappeared forever, and I would have remained a nonentity. It is still inconceivable to me that recordings of so many superb performances could have been deliberately destroyed; and imagine how much money might have been made by selling copies of these archival gems ...

45

Maria Cebotari

IT WAS IN THE EARLY 1940s that I first heard of Maria Cebotari, a brilliant Russian singer born in Moldavia – a small country, once independent but later under Russian rule. During the Revolution she fled to Germany, where she made her career in the 1930s. She also became a member of the famous Vienna Staatsoper. I was deeply saddened to learn that she died very tragically of cancer in 1949 while in her prime as a singer. But that, as far as I was concerned, was the end of the story.

In 1995 an extremely shy and retiring neighbour of mine, called Alasdair Henderson, stayed for supper after kindly fitting a new lock to my pantry. My first CD had recently been released, and on being told about it he hesitantly asked me if I had heard of Maria Cebotari. He mispronounced her surname, and it took me some time to recognize it. When I did, I was astonished, and asked how he could possibly know of a name so completely outside his normal orbit.

He rather diffidently replied that Cebotari's son was his closest friend, and that he was the photographer Fritz Curzon. They had attended the same school and university together, and Fritz, who now lived in Canterbury, often stayed at Alasdair's flat, using it as a *pied-à-terre*. In fact he was staying at the flat that very night. I thought at the time that Alasdair was rambling and that the conversation had taken a slightly offbeat direction, but it suddenly started to take shape, and what I heard left me open-mouthed.

Maria Cebotari's husband, the famous Austrian film actor, Gustav Diessl, had died a year before she did, and the couple left behind them two small boys. Fritz was then two and a half years old, and his brother four. A trust fund had been set up for them, and they were left in the care of their nanny, who worshipped them. At this particular time, one of Britain's most famous pianists, Clifford Curzon, and his American wife began to think about adopting a child. Through the grapevine Curzon heard about the two boys, now living in Vienna. Although seemingly the most English of gentlemen, he was actually an Austrian and had a property in that country where he often took respites between his concerts.

He was about to leave for Austria, and organized a meeting with the boys. He then took them away for a few days to see whether they would bond together, after which he decided to adopt them. Because their nanny unfortunately seemed to be obsessively possessive, it was agreed to leave her behind when they left for England. The poor woman, bereft of all she loved, later drowned herself – a deeply sad note to an otherwise happy resolution. Having told me this story, Alasdair asked to hear my new CD. When I explained that my CD player was not working properly, he offered to take it to Fritz, who would look at it for me.

Early the following morning my doorbell rang. On opening the door I saw a tall, elegant gentleman carrying my CD player. It was Fritz Curzon, and by an odd coincidence, he looked not unlike Clifford Curzon as I remembered him. He joined me at breakfast, and soon we were chatting like old friends. He was married to the daughter of Michael Hordern, the actor, and they had two children. It was interesting to hear his own version of the events related by Alasdair; until fairly recently Maria Cebotari had been only a name to him, and a person whose image he remembered only vaguely, if at all. He had had a very happy and interesting childhood with Clifford Curzon and his wife, and when he was not studying, he had been involved in the backstage life of his father's international concert profession.

About a year after Fritz's first visit to my flat (he often came to see me between his photographic assignments) my great friend Richard Samuel was persuaded to join the Organization for Security and Co-Operation in Europe, in an advisory capacity. He became head of OSCE's mission in Moldavia in 1994 and spent some time in that country. On his return to London he visited me, and suddenly announced rather despairingly that he had been asked by the Moldavian president to do something seemingly impossible: to find one or both of Maria Cebotari's sons. Since Moldavia's independence from Russia, the country was seeking a figurehead, and the most apt person was the late Maria Cebotari. They wanted to honour her by honouring her children; streets were going to be named after her, and they wanted her descendants to play their part in the celebrations.

Richard had tried every possible avenue and had drawn blanks. The only clue he had been given was that their name was now Curzon. Having given the Moldavian president his promise of finding the boys, he felt desperately inadequate. I let him ramble on before very casually saying, 'Shall I ring Fritz so that you can pass all this on to him?' At first he did not take in what I was saying, and when I repeated my offer, the astonishment on his face was beyond description. I phoned Fritz and handed the receiver to Richard; and so a small piece of Moldavian history was born that day in London w14.

When more and more historic CDs of long-ago artists started to be released a few years back, Maria Cebotari lived again. And by the strangest twist of fate, her CDs were released by the same company as mine – Preiser. In September 1998 Fritz and his family flew to Kichinev, capital of Moldavia, and spent five days being treated like royalty with a hospitality that left them speechless. The main street leading to the president's palace is now called after Maria Cebotari, as are various buildings in the city.

46

Recording Again – and Writing

I T NEEDED A TREMENDOUS amount of courage to make the final decision. Having made it, I still shook with apprehension. To record again, and to make a new CD at the age of eighty-one, could have seemed not only like black comedy but also rather heady. Yet my voice simply seemed to demand it, so I went along with the idea.

It all started the previous year, 1996, with my first pupil. Recalling the wonderful scales and exercises that I had once used for my own needs, I sang them to her, only to discover that, after a total silence of thirty-two years, my voice was still very much there. If I may say so, it was almost as pleasing and flexible as before. Tsivi Sharret, a delightful young pianist and accompanist, heard me give a lesson and asked me to allow her to work with me. I was astonished by this request, and asked her what she wanted to work with me on. 'Your singing', she replied. When I told her that I did not sing at all, she started to 'manipulate' me and brainwash me into brushing up my voice, which had been silent for such a long time.

At that time I had no piano, but a kind neighbour offered us the use of hers. So twice a week Tsivi and I would go off to practice together and to recycle what was still there in the voice. At the end of practically every session I would laugh bitterly, recognizing the absurdity of what I was doing. I would then declare, 'Right! That's it. I'm not prepared to go on making a fool of myself by singing scales at the age of eighty. Enough is enough.' Tsivi would fold her hands on her lap, look at me with her huge, lugubrious brown eyes, and say in her melting accent, 'Kyra, don't be selfish. You still have a lot to give to the world.' This remark always cut me to the quick, and so I always replied, 'Okay, just *once* more.'

As these 'once mores' continued, my repertoire of light music grew and grew. Tsivi – and other people – started nagging me to make a new CD, thereby challenging me to do what was logically impossible. In addition to my continuing awareness of the ridiculous situation I had put myself in, I was suffering acutely from a displaced hip, and every step was agony. However, we made a short trial tape, and the result was so amazing – so unusual, so *personal* –

that I agreed to start working towards a full CD. Everyone's enthusiasm boosted my own, and suddenly I was recording for real.

My choice of items was simple: nothing beyond the current range and limits of my voice and, therefore, no vocal risks. The songs were nostalgic time capsules recalling days gone by, and the idea was to create the sort of crossover album that unfortunately would have been unacceptable in my day. Some of the items I had sung in my twenties, others I always longed to sing but had never had the opportunity to do so. There was a feisty Purcell song, Victorian drawing-room ditties, schmalzy German and glitzy French waltzes, Russian songs (so close to my heart, and sung in my own individual way), and two hitherto unrecorded songs by Michael White, a prolific but rarely-heard composer of the 1930s and 1940s. I also chose a Verlaine poem set to music by Earl Okin who, after all, had set the ball rolling by persuading Preiser to release my first two CDs of old recordings.

Although I had to sit, in some pain, for the sessions, hey presto! it was suddenly all done. The result was my first studio recording, *Nostalgia with Kyra Vayne*. But – and it was a big but – I started to panic when the date of the disc's completion and release approached. I could so easily be ridiculed and slated, even dismissed completely, and how would I cope with that? Fortunately I shall never know, because the opposite happened: the object of the CD was understood by the critics, and I received glowing reviews.

Nostagia has flaws, of course. How could it not? But I sincerely hope that these are forgiven and overlooked in the face of those other moments of (I trust) enchantment. Listening to the disc as an outsider – I stress once again that my opinion is completely objective – I am amazed at what an eighty-one year old voice can still achieve and express.

*

For years, many people had suggested that I write a book about my life. When my first CD was released in 1995 this innocent request gradually swelled into a large clamour, and it caused me not only to reflect on incidents from my past but also to think how these could be arranged to give shape to a life that had always seemed, to me, a total mess. My impression of my life had been generally negative, with a strong conviction of having spent perhaps three-quarters of it sitting around and waiting for Godot; but once I allowed my mind to wind its way backwards through time, I was almost bewildered by how much had actually taken place.

The first task was to start putting episodes down on paper.

Having rid myself of a very good electric typewriter when I retired from secretarial work, I was forced to write longhand; and although a number of people offered to help me, they would either rewrite my words to suit their own ego or let me down because of the pressures of their own work. I always acknowledged that I needed help with the book, and I believed that somewhere there was the Right Person for the task, but it was a matter of looking and waiting for him or her to come along. And it often seemed that time was running out.

Then I suddenly realized that a young man from Nottingham, who had come to interview me for his forthcoming book on divas, was that person. We had a rapport, and he was eager to further the writing career for which he was fully qualified. His name was Andrew Palmer, and this book is the result of our collaboration. Our working relationship has been most amicable, and he has in no way taken over the project. On the contrary, he has simply given the book an overall structure, corrected certain things, and offered a number of ideas, while ensuring that my individual style of writing has remained intact.

I should explain that I have excised from the manuscript a number of incidents in my life, either because they were too convoluted to recount or because I felt they would appear too incredible. Even so, I myself still find what I have written in these pages almost unbelievable. It is, however, all absolutely true.

I am very happy to have completed − at last − the book that so many people wanted me to write. In doing so, I have rounded off another circle in my life. And I am fortunate in having as my publishers Arcadia Books, a youthful but highly successful company courageously founded only a few years ago by Gary Pulsifer − yes! he of the trip to Russia that took place just before my rebirth. I am sure ours will be a most happy association.

47

Furry Friends

THIS BOOK would not be complete without a few words on the subject of my real passion: animals. I adore them all – truly, madly, deeply – and feel sorry for anyone who does not know the joys that they bring. They ask for so little, and yet give so much.

Over the years I have had thirteen cats, not including my current duo, and one dog. I suppose I adore dogs even more than cats, if that were possible, but as they are far less independent, they need a more regular life and more physical attention. The dog that I promised myself on retirement never materialized, but then I have never *really* retired, and seem to have had one occupation after another. However, I am on personal terms with every dog in our village in West London, and often find myself almost tipped over by one who has recognized my posterior and who makes no bones about letting me know!

In fact, I know the local dogs much better than their owners. On one occasion when I had taken one of my felines to the Blue Cross for a check-up, a young man came up to me as I was leaving the surgery, cat-basket with cat in my hand. He asked me whether I was mobile or whether I had come by public transport; and when I replied, 'Public transport', he asked if he could give me a lift home, explaining that he lived very near me. I said rather warily, 'Thank you very much, but do I know you?' He replied, 'Well, not exactly, but you do know my *dog!*'

I have had four Siamese cats: Rani, Fred, Vanya, and Macchu (whose brother, Picchu, was run over while a very small kitten). The last two were named after their first owner's honeymoon in Mexico, and an asthmatic baby – the result of the marriage – sent Macchu in my direction. He arrived with a trousseau that only a cat like him – one with everything – could possibly bring.

Tobias 1, Tobias 2, and Tobias 3 were all tabby and white, and there was a tortoiseshell, or 'tortie', who looked so like an owl that she became known as Sovoushka (Russian for 'owlet'). There was also a magical Burmese, named Olechka; and Blossom, a long-haired Birman, regal beyond words, who ate only in my bedroom, away from the riff-raff, and *only* fresh steak. In old age he had a wanderlust, often disappearing but always being rescued in the nick of time, just as my heart was finally breaking; and he always returned with a look of accusation as to why it had taken so long to be reclaimed. Doushkin, another little tabby, appeared to only tolerate me, but he would always be waiting for me, no matter how, or from where, I arrived home – at any hour of the day or night.

All my cats had adventurous lives and were amazing characters. They were all homeless or unwanted before they crossed my path, and except for two, they all went into their final, blissful sleep cradled in my arms – the last gift I could give them, and the best. If only I had a vet to see *me* on my way ...

My present cats, Nicholas (Nicky) and Dmitri (Dima), are superb. The former was once a minute, lost and unweaned mite who adopted me, but he is now an enormous black and white, longhaired young man with huge, questioning, gold eyes and whiskers to beat all whiskers. His nickname, in fact, is Clark Gable. Dima is a slim and elegant silver tabby, independent beyond decency but very satisfied with what fate has dealt him. And I have a visiting neighbour: Shadow, a one-year old with pure black fur like a seal, who comes in search of Dima. His squeak is almost extra-terrestrial, and somehow Dima always wakes up eagerly, even if fast asleep, long before the catflap flaps to signal Shadow's arrival.

As for horses ... To me, their beauty is unsurpassable in the animal kingdom. *If* I were ever to worship anything, it would be at the shrine of Equus.

48

Success?

WHY DID I NEVER BECOME A MEGASTAR? Although this question has often been asked of me, and although I have given the matter a great deal of thought, it remains difficult to answer conclusively. However, I think the principal reason was my deep sense of insecurity – or rather, a lack of realistic self-evaluation. What I have already written about my childhood and youth should explain, to a great extent, why I had very few expectations from life. Thanks to the appalling conditions in Russia at that time, and my early days in London, I grew up feeling like a second-class citizen. I accepted this – to have demanded more in those circumstances would have been pointless, even obstreperous – and I lived accordingly. What little *did* come my way was simply welcomed.

As I grew older I realized that with a different mentality I could have put my assets to great advantage. But sadly, I had an over-developed sense of right and wrong that governed everything I did. Moreover, my family background was characterized by fitful quarrelling between my parents and with my sister, and because I loathed this I suppose I always tried to avoid conflict when I was older. When I did lash out verbally, my tongue could be very harsh indeed – and the consequences dire. So whenever I could, I kept my mouth shut.

The greatest professional mistake I made was to put myself so completely in the hands of my impresario, Eugene Iskoldoff. But having done so, I had to give myself, and him, a chance. My apparent submissiveness was actually a form of despair, of giving in, because I seemed unable to play a winning card myself. I know that my voice should have been a trump card – in fact, the one to trump all trumps – but in an artist's career, luck and the psychological moment need to coincide. In my case, they did not. My career took the wrong course right from the beginning – the recipe was certainly there, but most of the ingredients were missing.

One important factor was that I bypassed – or was bypassed by – oratorio singing. After qualifying at a music academy, most singers of that period were thrown straight into oratorio, and it provided a superb shop window for their talents as well as a constant means of earning money from their voices. But I had no such academic background. For example, my archaic school's curriculum offered no cultural input whatsoever, and so I never encountered anything like music appreciation. As a result, when I began my career, the world of oratorio lay completely outside my horizons.

I suppose that, after a while, I saw Gene as a 'cushion' or means of protection against the demands that would have been made on me by my profession. This compensated for the problems that our relationship created. And of course there was always the hope that my career would suddenly turn the corner ... It is hard to explain, but I have always been very sensitive about my voice, feeling that it should be treated as something special and fragile, and I therefore believed that it should not be adulterated by the sordidness that was so strong a component of artistic life. However, I was wrong. Compromises have to be made.

Often I failed to assert myself against impossibly obstinate people, for obstinacy is something that I have never had the capacity or inclination to fight against. As I have already suggested, I was inordinately conscious of my lack of formal qualifications, and I therefore needed someone who cared sufficiently to point out to me that *real* talent is the only qualification necessary. But here again, the front that I created for myself probably went before me and concealed my inner qualms. I must have appeared much more confident than I actually was.

What I required was an agent, ambitious to build his reputation on my talent. But it is often hard to see the wood for the trees, and to be on the inside looking out often distorts one's view. In retrospect I can see that an impresario like Gene would be ambitious to build *himself* up by organizing large, spectacular shows and lavish spectacles. This is why he used me as a catalyst for his own fulfilment. I never understood why he refused to take on other artists, but of the course the reason is that he would then have been an agent, not an impresario.

I encountered further obstacles through not being part of the musical establishment. For example, when Gene started negotiations to bring the Italian Opera Company over to England, Covent Garden interpreted this as 'trespassing on their territory' and were most displeased. They demanded to vet our repertoire so that it would not clash with theirs, and they did everything in their power to prevent the artists in question obtaining entry visas. In the end it was Richard Attenborough and the late Peter Daubeny who used their influence to resolve the situation, but the fact that I was the only Brit to sing with the Italian Opera Company did not endear me to Covent Garden or to the rest of the establishment. In those days, attitudes were much narrower and more insular; today, the artistic world has broadened enormously, and the establishment as such has all but disappeared. Talent is grabbed by the highest bidder, regardless of its nationality – or, perhaps, because of it.

Another incident from that period speaks for itself. When ENSA came into being, around 1940, it was divided into two sections: Classical, headed by Walter Legge, and Variety, run by Bob Lecardo. I naturally auditioned for Legge, who wished to engage me there and then. When I explained that I was bound by a contract that still had some time to run, he suggested that I have dinner with a certain gentleman and 'stay for breakfast.' This, he explained, was the easiest way to resolve the problem. I immediately understood the inference, thanked him, went to the Variety section, and got in with no strings attached. Afterwards I was grateful not to have become involved with Walter Legge; he was a cruel and dominating man.

Yet another important factor in my lack of professional progress was the absence, at that time, of prestigious voice competitions. One of the first such contests was the Geneva International Singing Competition of 1947, which was won by Victoria de los Angeles. She was signed up by a very powerful Parisian agent, Leonidov, who 'bought' a performance of *La Bohème* for her in France, and she therefore made it to the top with her first operatic engagement. However, it was very difficult to enter the Geneva competition, and it did not run for long. Today, in contrast, it is essential for *every* musician – whether an instrumentalist or a singer – to win a competition (and not necessarily the First Prize) in order to make a career. Competing is both a prerequisite and an enormous incentive, and it certainly sorts out the wheat from the chaff.

Nor were there sponsorships in those days, for the concept was only just starting to be initiated. Today, sponsorship is a fact of artistic life for both individuals and corporations. There are also far more opera companies now than during my career – in those days, there was only Covent Garden, Sadlers Wells, and the Carl Rosa. Nor were amateur groups taken seriously, as they are today. Indeed, for any present-day singer with talent, there are numerous amateur and semi-professional companies that provide the kind of effective grounding that was unavailable when I began my career.

The recording industry, too, has changed and developed enormously. CDs have become a way of life, and artists today often make a name for themselves on disc before appearing in the flesh. Some of them are also headhunted, whereas in my time, singers such as Claudia Muzio and Oda Slobodskaya paid for their own recordings at the end of their careers – the hunting came from the artists, not from the record companies. My own, late recognition proves the importance of recordings: with one CD, my name was made – for a selective audience. Following the release of my second disc, my name grew and was known by a much wider audience: *Desert Island Discs*, *Kaleidoscope*, *Woman's Hour*, Welsh radio, New Zealand radio, Washington *Niteline* and the Toronto press all featured me. This, of course, was in addition to the wide coverage that the British national press gave me.

I had no media contacts of my own, and success came to me while sitting at home, without my having to lift the proverbial finger. I have nevertheless made what could be called a global career, and Kyra Vayne has become almost a household name. If only it had been a quarter as easy at the beginning of my career. If only. The power of a small plastic disc, together with willing ears (plus a little talent, of course!) . . . those were the crucial ingredients.

Epilogue

I CONSIDER MYSELF fortunate in that I have been able to look at my rebirth completely objectively. Had I not, my sanity might easily have been in jeopardy. The first shocks (for such they were) came so unexpectedly and irregularly that my spirits yo-yoed, soaring one day and crashing the next. There seemed to be no in-between, and after each high I would lapse into deep, dark depression. But eventually the waves of elation and despondency evened out, and a balance was acquired. I now realize how very privileged I am, and I feel a deep sense of gratitude for what has happened. Above all, I now know who I am.

Today I am surrounded by many wonderful friends, to most of whom I suspect I am two different people: the down-to-earth Kyra, with her fruity and slightly bawdy sense of the ridiculous; and the opera diva Kyra Vayne, owner of a precious and individual instrument. I have a large and loyal band of *aficionados* throughout the world, and I am amazed that in the midst of today's media sleaze and hype of singers – both classical and pop, who are now also known as divas – there is still room for me and for my voice. To me, this is perhaps the greatest source of wonder.

I am grateful that, despite all of life's wonderful ups and appalling downs, I am still sane enough to savour to the full the fruits of a talent given to me so generously. And I remain proud of the integrity that went with it. There is, ultimately, a feeling of having won – or rather, of my *voice* having won. It remained true to its philosophy, and simply waited.

Kyra Vayne Discography

Kyra Vayne (Preiser 89996)

Borodin:	Jaroslavna's Arioso and Complainte (*Prince Igor*)
Verdi:	Ernani!, Ernani, involami (*Ernani*)
Gluck:	O del mio dolce ardor (*Paride ed Elena*)
Boito:	L'altra notte in fondo al mare (*Mefistofele*)
Tchaikovsky:	Lisa's Aria (*Pique Dame*)
Spontini:	Impitoyables dieux! (*La Vestale*)
Puccini:	Vissi d'arte (*Tosca*)
Verdi:	Pace, pace, mio Dio (*La Forza del Destino*)
Schubert:	Im Frühling
Tchaikovsky:	Christ In His Garden, Op.54
	To Forget So Soon
	Life's Morning
Mussorgksy:	Cradle Song
	We Parted Proudly
	By The Don
Glière:	The Lark
Grechaninov:	Epicedium
Rachmaninov:	Lilacs, Op.21
	Sing not to me, beautiful maiden, Op.4
	Spring Waters, Op.14

Kyra Vayne, Volume 2 (Preiser 89993)

Tchaikovsky:	Tatiana's Letter Scene (*Eugene Onegin*)
Kochetov:	The Night Is Warm
Grechaninov:	When Softly Sighs the Golden Corn
Vasilenko:	The Spirit Of My Love Returns To Me
	Rani, Beloved One
Mussorgksy:	Parassia's Aria and Khivria's Aria (*The Fair of Sorochintsi*)
Szymanowski:	The Beloved's Death (Songs of the Infatuated Muezzin)
Berlioz:	La Mort de Cléopâtre
Wagner:	Senta's Ballade (*Der Fliegende Holländer*)
Puccini:	Quando m'en vò (*La Bohème*)
Provost:	Intermezzo
Bach-Gounod:	Ave Maria
Lehár:	Vilja-Lied (*Die Lustige Witwe*)
Johann Strauss II:	Czárdás (*Die Fledermaus*)

Kyra Vayne (Eklipse EKR P-16)

Spontini:	Excerpts from *La Vestale*
Verdi:	Ernani!, Ernani, involami (*Ernani*)
Puccini:	Vissi d'arte (*Tosca*)
Verdi:	Miserere (*Il Trovatore*)

Verdi:	Pace, pace, mio Dio (*La Forza del Destino*)
Mussorgsky:	The Ragamuffin
Prokofiev:	The Ugly Duckling
Adrian Foley:	One Night In Old Seville
Philip Kadman:	The Sea Without a Shore (*Amarak*)
Trad.:	Gori, Gori/Black Eyes (Medley)

Nostalgia With Kyra Vayne (Eklipse EKR P-19)

Alexander Hume:	Afton Water
Balfe:	I dreamt I dwelt in marble halls (*The Bohemian Girl*)
Michael White:	A Fairy Went a'Marketing
	Close Thine Eyes
Sigmund Romberg:	When I grow too old to dream
Heyman:	Live, Love, Laugh (after Johann Strauss)
Hollander:	Ich weiss nicht (*Stürme der Liedenschaft*)
Kosma:	Autumn Leaves
Michel Legrand:	The Windmills of Your Mind
Purcell:	Man Is For Woman Made
Earl Okin:	La bonne chanson
Offenbach:	Ah! quel dîner je viens de faire! (*La Périchole*)
Poulenc:	Les Chemins de l'amour
Oscar Strauss:	C'est la saison de l'amour (*Les Trois Valses*)
Kovan:	I Want
Trad. Russian tango:	Who Knows?
Trad.:	My Heart
	Snow Flurries
Trad. Gypsy:	Burn, the Heart of a Gypsy
	Black Eyes
	The autumn wind is plaintively wailing
	At The Gate
Grechaninov:	Cradle Song (recorded in 1935 and 1997)

INDEX

Andrew Palmer is a freelance writer who specialises in classical music and musicians. His work has appeared on national radio (BBC Radio 3) and in the international music press, and since 1997 he has been a contributor to *Strings* magazine (USA).

He holds degrees in Communication Studies and Writing (MA) from Nottingham Trent University, where he teaches Writing and Social Sciences. He is currently editing the correspondence of William Alwyn for Toccata Press and writing *Divas ... In Their Own Words*, a book based on exclusive conversations with fifty famous sopranos and mezzo-sopranos.

When Memory Dies
A. Sivanandan

A three-generational saga of a Sri Lankan family's search for coherence and continuity in a country broken by colonial occupation and riven by ethnic wars. *Winner of the Sagittarius Prize 1998* and *shortlisted for the Commonwealth Writers Prize 1998.* FOURTH IMPRESSION.

'Haunting ... with an immense tenderness. The extraordinary poetic tact of this book makes it unforgettable' – John Berger, *Guardian*

The Last Kabbalist of Lisbon
Richard Zimler

A literary mystery set among secret Jews living in Lisbon in 1506 when, during Passover celebrations, some two thousand Jewish inhabitants were murdered in a pogrom. THE INTERNATIONAL BESTSELLER. NINTH IM-PRESSION.

'Remarkable erudition and compelling imagination, an American Umberto Eco' – Francis King, *Spectator*

Night Letters
Robert Dessaix

Every night for twenty nights in a hotel room in Venice, a man recently diagnosed with HIV writes a letter home to a friend. He describes not only the kaleidoscopic journey he has just made from Switzerland across north-ern Italy to Venice, but reflects on questions of mortality, seduction and the search for paradise.

'Dessaix writes with great elegance, with passion, compassion, and sly wit. Literally a wonderful book' – John Banville

Double Act
Fiona Pitt-Kethley

'This poetry collection reads like it's been written by a sexually charged Philip Larkin. Both witty and scathing, it avoids the tender eroticism often employed when discussing sex and instead goes straight for the jugular'
– D›tour *Magazine*

Time Exposure
Brodrick Haldane
in conversation with Roddy Martine

For almost six decades Brodrick Haldane moved among the rich and the famous, photographing everybody who was anybody, including the Queen Mother, Bernard Shaw, the Aga Khan and Margaret, Duchess of Argyll. *Time Exposure* is a witty and charming portrait of an age peopled by extraordinary characters.

'The original society paparazzo, snapping the Duke of Windsor and Wallis Simpson in exile, Charlie Chaplin and a youthful JFK' – *Sunday Times*

False Light
Peter Sheldon
Foreword by Francis King

Karl is a handsome adolescent in Vienna between the wars. He has every advantage, but all is not as it seems in a situation full of political tensions and erotic undercurrents.

'An absorbing read' – Sebastian Beaumont, *Gay Times*

Eurydice in the Underworld
Kathy Acker

The last work of new fiction Acker published before her death from breast cancer in late 1997, *Eurydice* is Acker's response to her diagnosis. Its 'raw truth is shot through with surprising lyricism and tenderness' – *Observer*. The collection also includes Acker classics such as 'Lust', 'Algeria' and 'Immoral', on the banning in Germany of *Blood and Guts in High School*.

'Kathy Acker's writing is virtuoso, maddening, crazy, so sexy, so painful, and beaten out of a wild heart that nothing can tame. Acker is a landmark writer' – Jeanette Winterson